Thomas Balinger

150 CHILDREN'S SONGS
FOR GUITAR

Other titles by Thomas Balinger:

All Time Classics for Guitar

The Ukulele Songbook – 50 All Time Classics
The Ukulele Songbook – 50 All Time Classics, Vol. II
The Ukulele Songbook – Best of Gospel
The Ukulele Songbook – Hymns and Songs of Worship
The Ukulele Songbook – Christmas carols
The Ukulele Songbook – Shanties and Songs of the sea

Most wanted Ukulele Chords

Thomas Balinger
150 Children's Songs for Guitar

thomasbalinger@gmail.com

© 2016

ISBN: 978-1530022922

Dear fellow guitar players,

here it is, my big collection of children's songs, nursery rhymes and lullabies for guitar. If you like to make music for and with children and you're looking for some songs to play, this is the book for you - and with a 150 songs to choose from, it'll take some time before you run out of songs to play.

All songs have been arranged for easy guitar with the beginning to intermediate player in mind; the ones that are somewhat harder to play can be mastered with only a little practice.

To make playing them as easy as possible, the songs have been transposed to „guitar-friendly" keys and feature melody notation plus chord symbols and full lyrics. I included chord diagrams next to each song, so you don't have to look up any chord - you can risk a quick glance even while playing. And if you don't know the melody of a particular song, don't worry: there's a melody TAB for each song to let you play the melody even if you don't read music.

Last not least I included an appendix. Here, you'll find tips on tuning your guitar plus a selection of strumming and picking patterns for song accompaniment and a handy compendium of basic guitar chords.

Wishing you lots of fun strumming, picking and singing these songs,
Thomas Balinger

Contents

Songs (in alphabetical order)

Appendix

Bobby Shafto

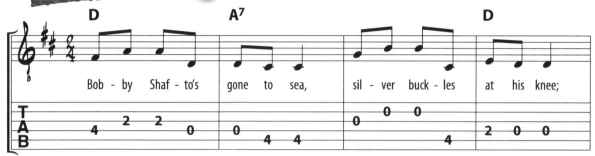

Bob - by Shaf - to's   gone to sea,   sil - ver buck - les   at his knee;

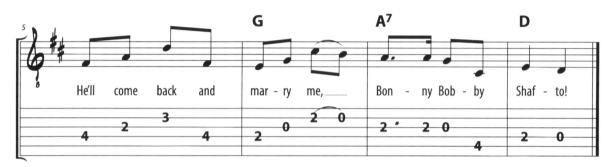

He'll   come   back   and   mar - ry me, ____   Bon - ny Bob - by   Shaf - to!

2. *Bobby Shafto's bright and fair,*
   panning out his yellow hair;
   He's my love for evermore,
   Bonny Bobby Shafto!

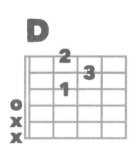

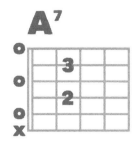

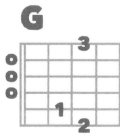

Bluebird, Bluebird

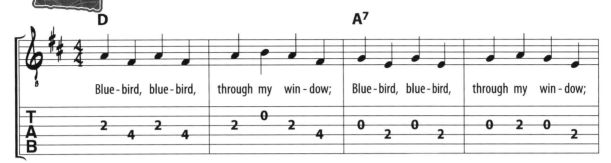

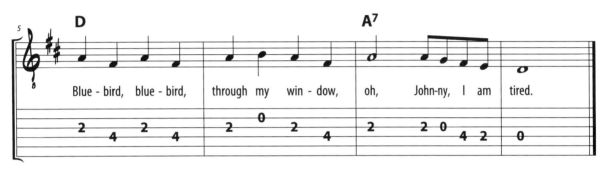

Blue-bird, blue-bird, through my win-dow; Blue-bird, blue-bird, through my win-dow;

Blue-bird, blue-bird, through my win-dow, oh, John-ny, I am tired.

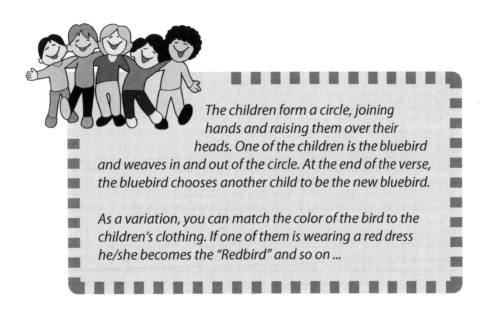

The children form a circle, joining hands and raising them over their heads. One of the children is the bluebird and weaves in and out of the circle. At the end of the verse, the bluebird chooses another child to be the new bluebird.

As a variation, you can match the color of the bird to the children's clothing. If one of them is wearing a red dress he/she becomes the "Redbird" and so on ...

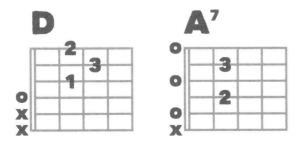

D   A^7

Grandfather's clock

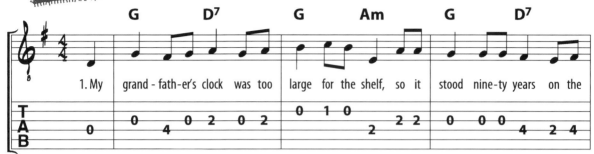

1. My grand-fath-er's clock was too large for the shelf, so it stood nine-ty years on the

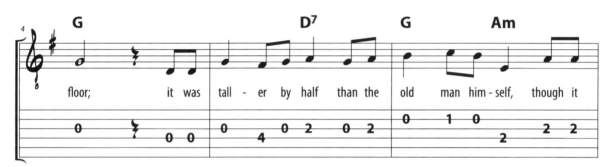

floor; it was tall-er by half than the old man him-self, though it

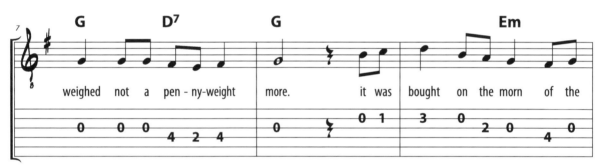

weighed not a pen-ny-weight more. it was bought on the morn of the

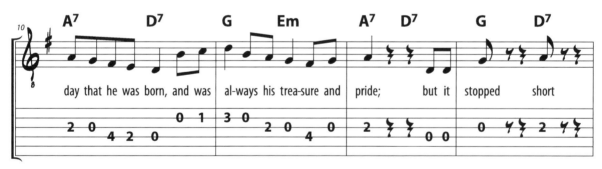

day that he was born, and was al-ways his trea-sure and pride; but it stopped short

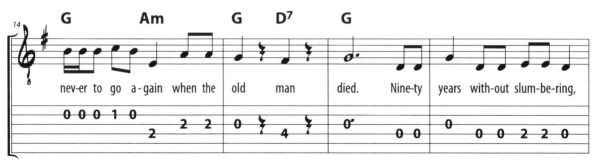

nev-er to go a-gain when the old man died. Nine-ty years with-out slum-ber-ing,

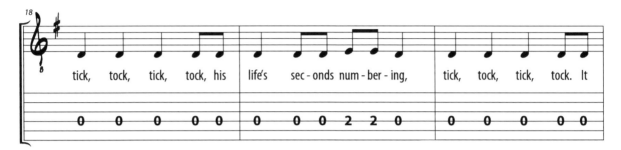

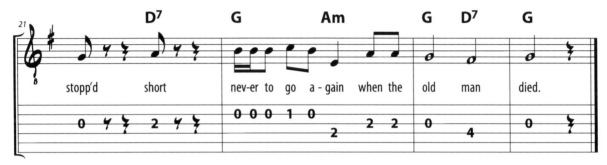

2. In watching its pendulum swing to and fro,
   many hours had he spent while a boy;
   and in childhood and manhood the clock
       seemed to know
   and to share both his grief and his joy.
   For it struck twenty-four when he entered
       at the door,
   With a blooming and beautiful bride;
   But it stopped short ...

3. My grandfather said that of those he could hire,
   not a servant so faithful he found;
   for it wasted no time, and had but one desire,
   at the close of each week to be wound.
   And it kept in its place not a frown upon its face,
   and its hands never hung by its side.
   But it stopped short ...

4. It rang an alarm in the dead of the night
   an alarm that for years had been dumb;
   and we knew that his spirit was pluming
       for flight
   that his hour of departure had come.
   Still the clock kept the time, with a soft
       and muffled chime,
   as we silently stood by his side;
   But it stopped short ...

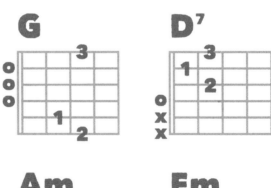

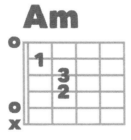

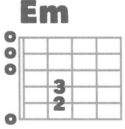

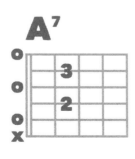

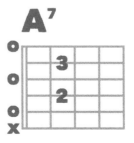

I love little kitty

I love lit-tle kit-ty, her coat is so warm, and if I don't hurt her, she'll

do me no harm. So I'll not pull her tail, nor

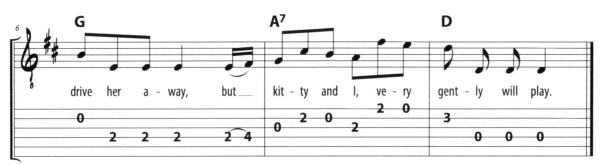

drive her a-way, but kit-ty and I, ve-ry gent-ly will play.

2. She shall sit by my side and I'll give her some food;
   And kitty will love me because I am good.
   I'll pat pretty kitty, and then she will purr;
   and thus show her thanks for my kindness to her.

3. I'll not pinch her ears, nor tread on her paw,
   lest I should provoke her to use her sharp claw.
   I never will vex her nor make her displeased:
   For kitty don't like to be worried and teased.

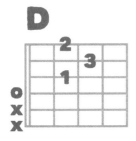
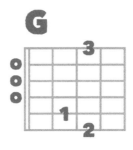
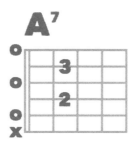

Five fat turkeys

Four fat turkeys are we ...
Three fat turkeys are we ...
Two fat turkeys are we ...

One fat turkey is me,
slept all night in a tree.
when the cook came around,
I couldn't be found,
so that's why I'm here you see!

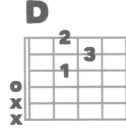

G

D

Sing quietly - the turkeys don't want to be found by the cook.

Sing loudly - the turkeys are proudly bragging about how they escaped the cook.

Sing slowly - the turkeys are tired.

Five little speckled frogs

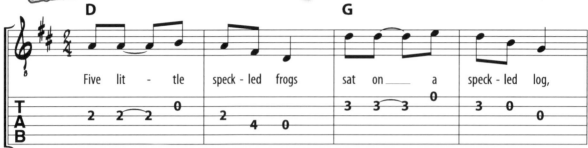

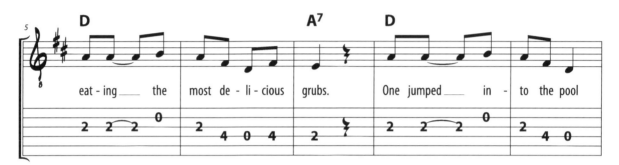

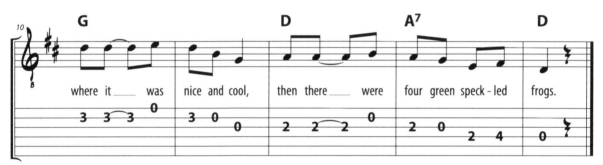

Four little speckled frogs …
Three little speckled frogs …
Two little speckled frogs …
One little speckled frog sat on a speckled log,
eating the most delicious grubs.
He jumped into the pool where it was nice and cool,
then there were no more speckled frogs.

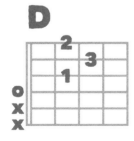

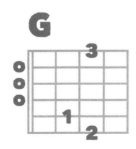

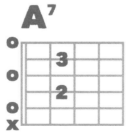

Golden slumbers

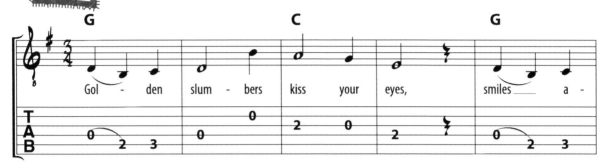

Gol - den slum - bers kiss your eyes, smiles ___ a -

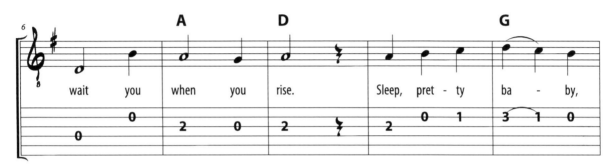

wait you when you rise. Sleep, pret - ty ba - by,

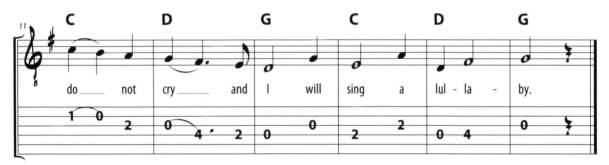

do ___ not cry ___ and I will sing a lul - la - by.

2. *Cares you know not, therefore sleep*
   while over you a watch I'll keep
   Sleep pretty darling, do not cry
   and I will sing a lullaby.

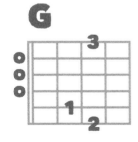
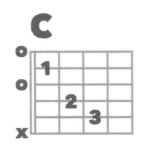
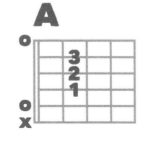
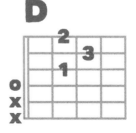

Winkum, winkum

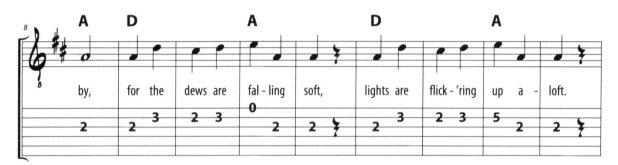

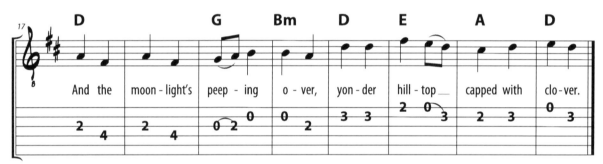

2. *Chickens long have gone to rest,*
   birds lie snug within their nest,
   and my birdie soon will be
   sleeping like a chick-a-dee.
   For with only half a try;
   Winkum, Winkum shuts her eye.

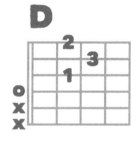

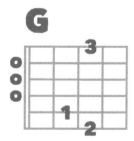

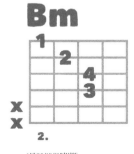

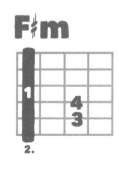

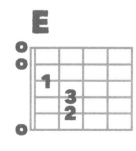

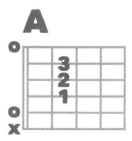

Wee Willi Winkie

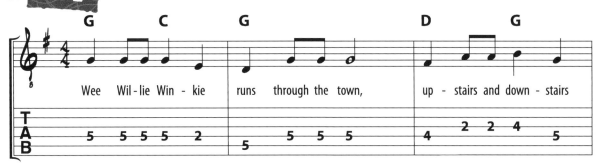

Wee Wil-lie Win-kie runs through the town, up - stairs and down - stairs

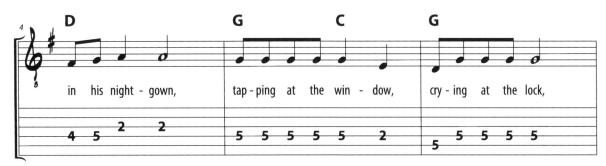

in his night - gown, tap-ping at the win - dow, cry - ing at the lock,

are the chil - dren in their bed, for it's past ten o'-clock?

The alphabet song

D				G		D		G		D		A		D
A	B	C	D	E	F	G,		H	I	J	K	L M N O		P.

TAB
```
              0  0              0  0                      2 2 2 2  0
        0  0     2  2                2           4  4
```

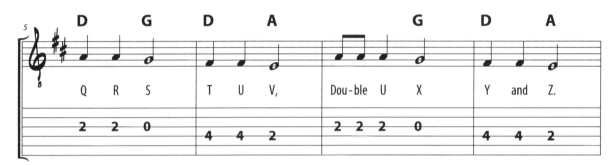

D	G	D	A		G	D	A
Q	R	S	T	U	V,	Dou-ble U X	Y and Z.

```
  2  2  0              2 2 2  0
           4  4  2              4  4  2
```

D		G	D	G	D	A	D
Now	I know my	A B	Cs,	won't you sing a -	long with me?		

```
              0  0              0  0
        0  0     2  2                2            4  4     2  2  0
```

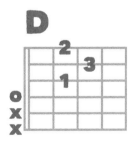

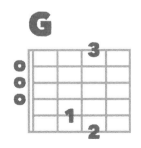

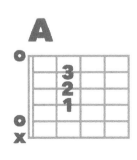

Simple Simon

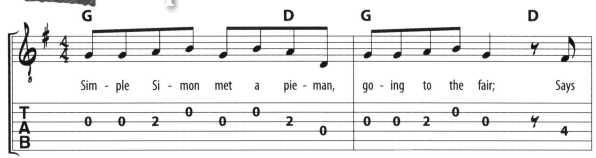

Sim - ple Si - mon met a pie - man, go - ing to the fair; Says

Sim - ple Si - mon to the pie - man, "Let me taste your ware". Says the man to Sim - ple Si - mon

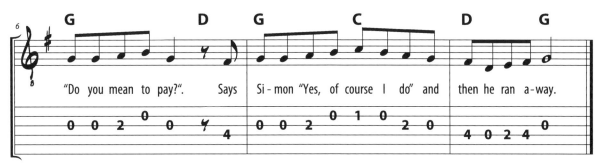

"Do you mean to pay?". Says Si - mon "Yes, of course I do" and then he ran a - way.

2. Simple Simon went a-fishing,
   for to catch a whale;
   All the water he had got,
   was in his mother's pail.

   Simple Simon went to look
   if plums grew on a thistle;
   He pricked his fingers very much,
   which made poor Simon whistle.

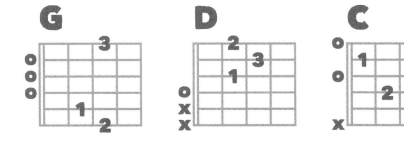

The fox

The fox went out on a chil-ly night, prayed to the Moon to

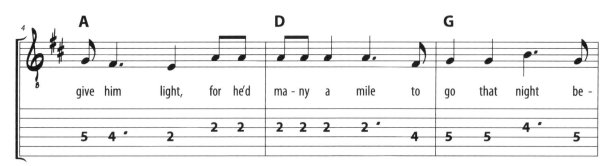

give him light, for he'd ma-ny a mile to go that night be-

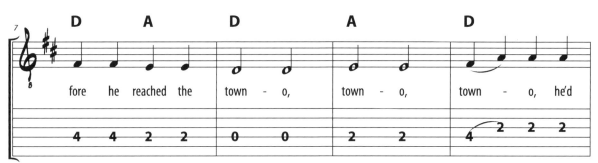

fore he reached the town - o, town - o, town - o, he'd

ma-ny a mile ___ to go that night be - fore he reached the town - o.

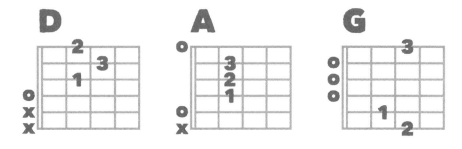

2. *He ran till he came to a great big pen*
   where the ducks and the geese were put therein.
   "A couple of you will grease my chin
   before I leave this town-o, town-o, town-o,
   a couple of you will grease my chin
   before I leave this town-o."

3. *He grabbed the grey goose by the neck,*
   throwed a duck across his back;
   he didn't mind their quack, quack, quack,
   and their legs all a-dangling down-o, down-o, down-o,
   he didn't mind their quack, quack, quack,
   and their legs all a-dangling down-o.

4. *Old Mother Flipper-Flopper jumped out of bed;*
   out of the window she cocked her head,
   Crying, "John, John! The grey goose is gone
   and the fox is on the town-o, town-o, town-o!"
   Crying, "John, John, the grey goose is gone
   and the fox is on the town-o!"

5. *Then John he went to the top of the hill,*
   blowed his horn both loud and shrill,
   the fox he said, "I'd better flee with my kill
   or they'll soon be on my trail-o, trail-o, trail-o."
   The fox he said, "I'd better flee with my kill
   or they'll soon be on my trail-o."

6. *He ran till he came to his cozy den;*
   there were the little ones eight, nine, ten.
   They said, "Daddy, better go back again,
   'cause it must be a mighty fine town-o, town-o, town-o!"
   They said, "Daddy, better go back again,
   'cause it must be a mighty fine town-o."

7. *Then the fox and his wife without any strife*
   cut up the goose with a fork and knife.
   They never had such a supper in their life
   and the little ones chewed on the bones-o, bones-o, bones-o,
   they never had such a supper in their life
   and the little ones chewed on the bones-o.

Sing a song of sixpence

Sing a song of six - pence, a pock-et full of rye, four and twen - ty black - birds,

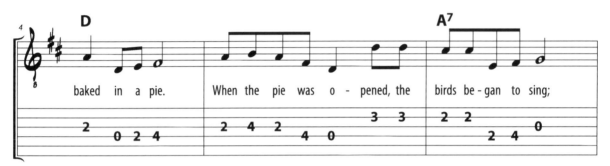

baked in a pie. When the pie was o - pened, the birds be - gan to sing;

Was - n't that a dain - ty dish to set be - fore the king?

2. *The king was in his counting house, counting out his money;*
   The queen was in the parlour, eating bread and honey.
   The maid was in the garden, hanging out the clothes,
   when down came a blackbird and pecked off her nose.

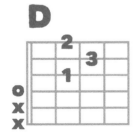

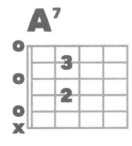

Hark, hark, the dogs do bark

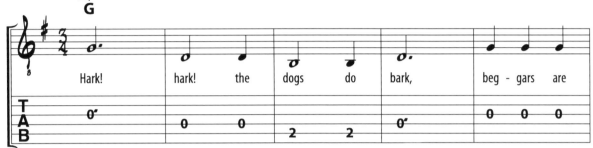

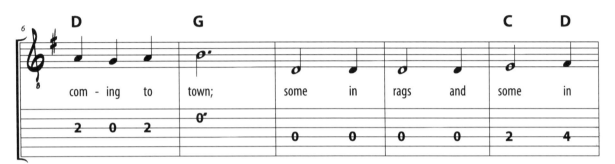

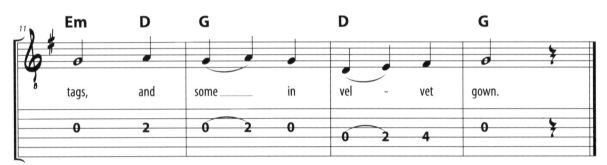

G | Hark! | hark! | the | dogs | do | bark, | beg - gars | are | com - ing | to | town; | some | in | rags | and | some | in | tags, | and | some | in | vel - vet | gown.

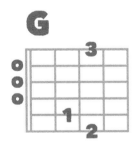

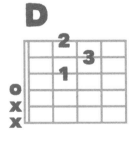

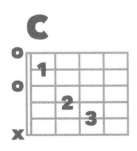

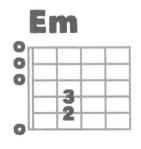

Little Polly Flinders

Lit - tle Pol - ly Flin - ders   sat a - mong the cin - ders,   warm - ing her pret - ty lit - tle

toes.   Her moth - er came and caught   her and   whipped her lit - tle daugh - ter for

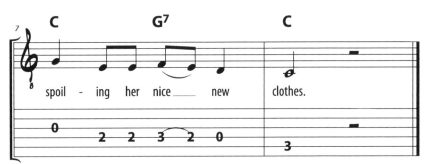

spoil - ing her nice ____ new   clothes.

Little Jack Horner

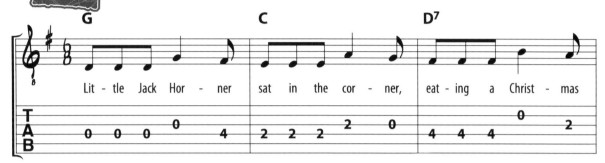

Lit - tle Jack Hor - ner   sat in the cor - ner,   eat - ing a Christ - mas

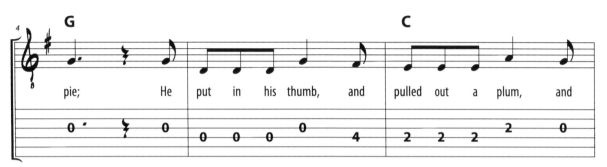

pie;   He   put in his thumb, and   pulled out a plum, and

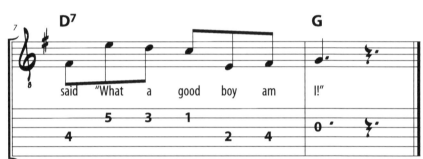

said "What a good boy am I!"

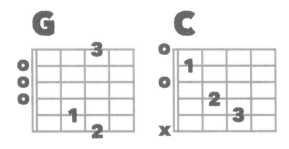

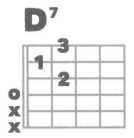

Old mother Hubbard

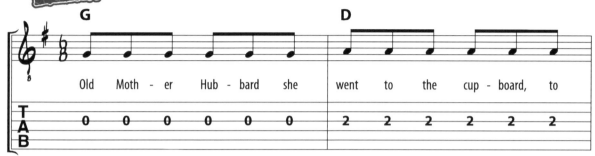

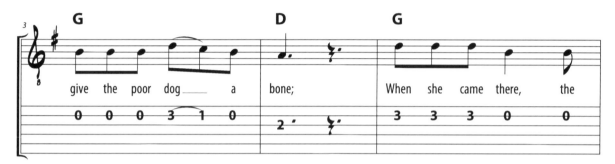

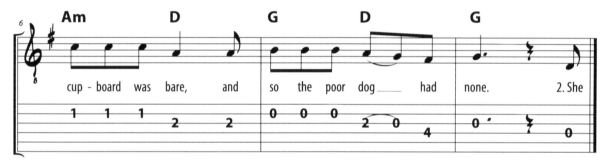

2. She went to the baker's to buy him some bread;
   When she came back the dog was dead!

3. She went to the undertaker's to buy him a coffin;
   When she came back the dog was laughing.

4. She took a clean dish to get him some tripe;
   When she came back he was smoking his pipe.

5. She went to the alehouse to get him some beer;
   When she came back the dog sat in a chair.

6. She went to the tavern for white wine and red;
   When she came back the dog stood on his head.

7. She went to the fruiterer's to buy him some fruit;
   When she came back he was playing the flute.

8. She went to the tailor's to buy him a coat;
    When she came back he was riding a goat.

9. She went to the hatter's to buy him a hat;
    When she came back he was feeding her cat.

10. She went to the barber's to buy him a wig
    When she came back he was dancing a jig.

11. She went to the cobbler's to buy him some shoes;
    When she came back he was reading the news.

12. She went to the sempstress to buy him some linen;
    When she came back the dog was spinning.

13. She went to the hosier's to buy him some hose;
    When she came back he was dressed in his clothes.

14. The Dame made a curtsy, the dog made a bow;
    The Dame said: "Your servant"; The dog said: "Bow-wow".

15. This wonderful dog was Dame Hubbard's delight,
    He could read, he could dance, he could sing, he could write.

16. She gave him rich dainties whenever he fed,
    And erected this monument when he was dead.

All night, all day

F ... B♭

All night, all ___ day, an-gels watch-ing o-ver

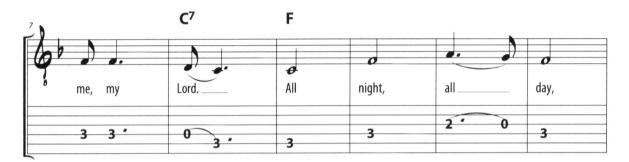

C⁷ ... F

me, my Lord. ___ All night, all ___ day,

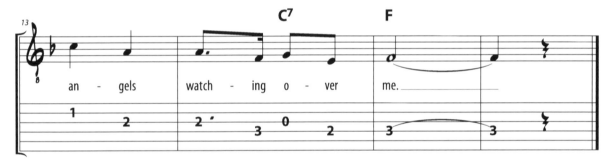

C⁷ ... F

an-gels watch-ing o-ver me. ___

2. When at night I go to sleep,
   angels watching over me, my Lord.
   Pray the Lord my soul to keep,
   angels watching over me.

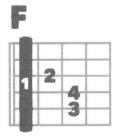

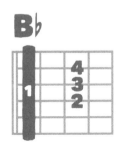

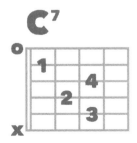

Cock a doodle do

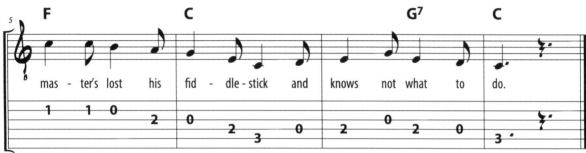

Cock a doo - dle do! My dame has lost her shoe, my

mas - ter's lost his fid - dle - stick and knows not what to do.

2. Cock a doodle do!
   What is my dame to do?
   Till master's found his fiddlingstick,
   She'll dance without her shoe.

3. Cock a doodle do!
   My dame has found her shoe,
   And master's found his fiddlingstick,
   Sing cock a doodle do!

4. Cock a doodle do!
   My dame will dance with you,
   While master fiddles his fiddlingstick,
   And knows not what to do.

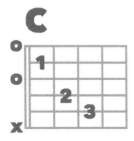

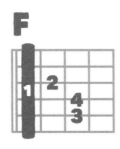

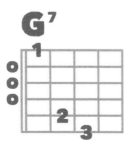

Star light, star bright

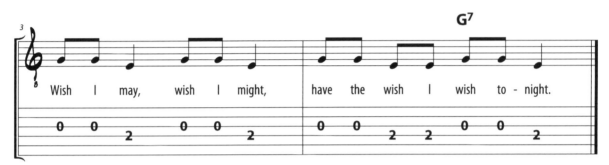

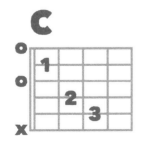
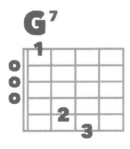

Christmas is coming

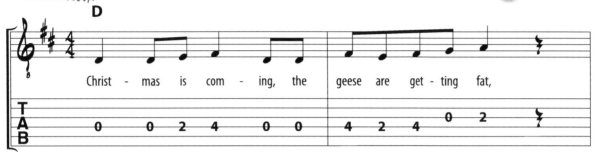

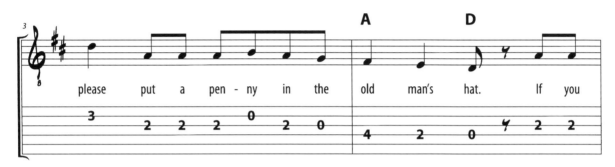

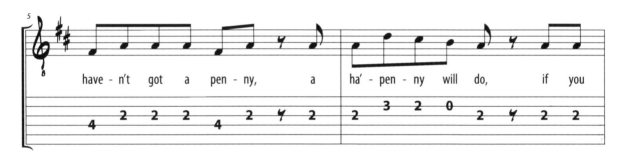

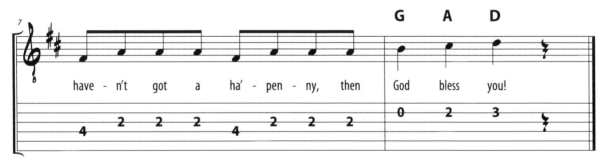

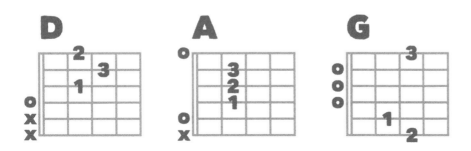

Here we go, looby loo

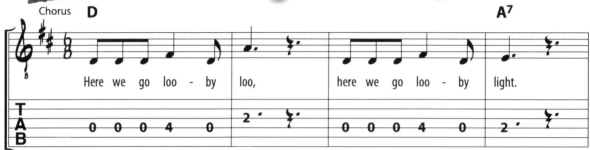

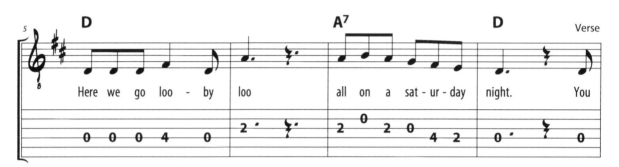

Chorus
D   A⁷

Here we go loo - by loo,   here we go loo - by light.

D   A⁷   D   Verse

Here we go loo - by loo   all on a sat - ur - day   night.   You

put   your   right   hand   in, _____   you   take   your   right   hand   out.   You

A⁷

give   your   right   hand   a   shake, shake, shake   and   turn   your-self   a - bout.

left hand ... right foot ... left foot ... head ... whole self ...

D   A⁷

Join hands and circle around during the chorus. During the verse, stop circling and do as the words indicate. After each verse, join hands and start circling again.

30

Boys and girls, come out to play

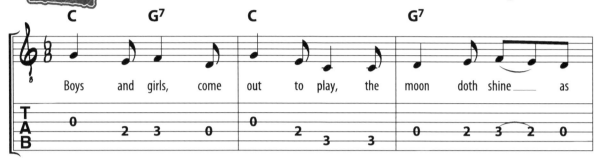

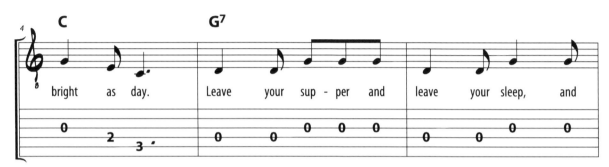

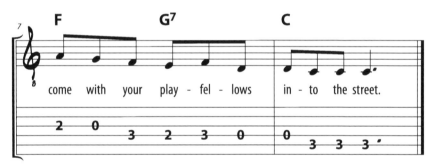

2. Come with a whoop, come with a call,
   come with a good will or not at all.
   Up the ladder and down the wall,
   a halfpenny roll will serve us all.

I had a little nut tree

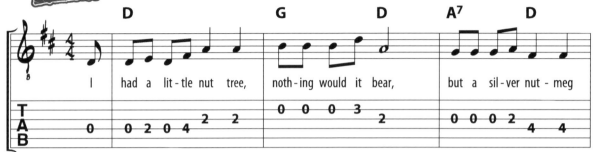

I had a lit - tle nut tree, noth - ing would it bear, but a sil - ver nut - meg

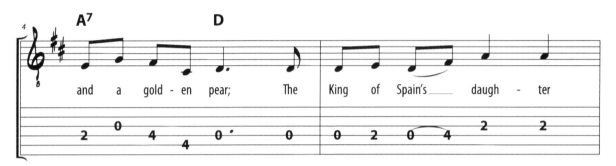

and a gold - en pear; The King of Spain's daugh - ter

came to vis - it me, and all for the sake of my lit - tle nut tree.

2. Her dress was made of crimson,
   jet black was her hair,
   she asked me for my nutmeg
   and my golden pear.

I said, "So fair a princess
never did I see,
I'll give you all the fruit
from my little nut tree."

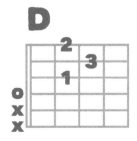
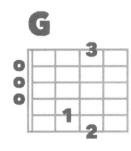
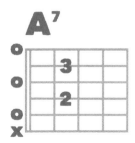

Miss Polly had a dolly

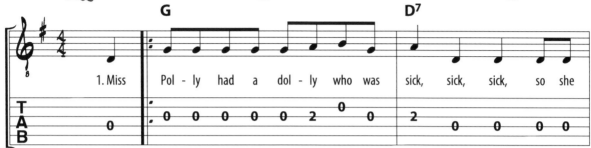

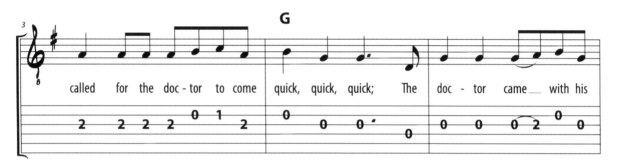

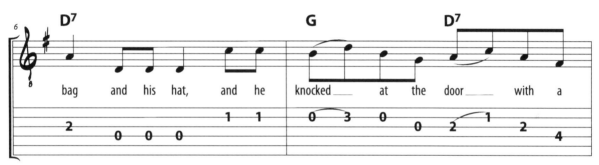

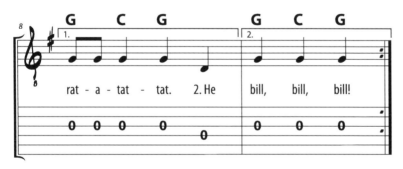

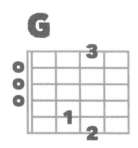

2. He looked at the dolly and he shook his head,
   And he said "Miss Polly, put her straight to bed."
   He wrote out a paper for a pill, pill, pill,
   "I'll be back in the morning with the bill, bill, bill!"

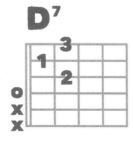

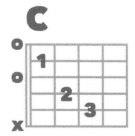

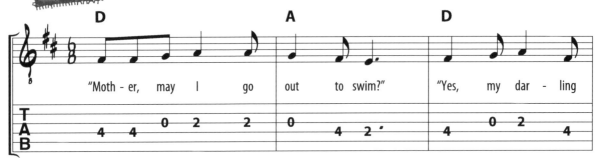

"Moth - er, may I go out to swim?" "Yes, my dar - ling

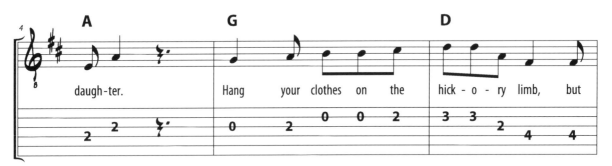

daugh-ter. Hang your clothes on the hick - o - ry limb, but

don't go near the wa - ter!"

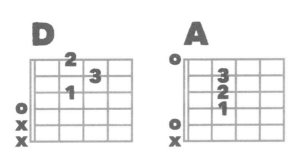

D   A

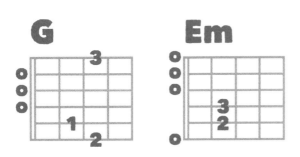

G   Em

Pussy-cat, Pussy-cat

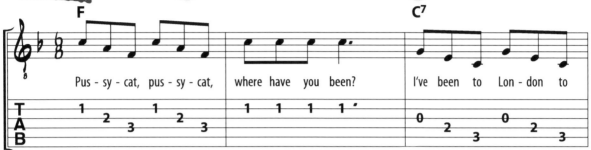

Pus - sy - cat, pus - sy - cat, where have you been? I've been to Lon - don to

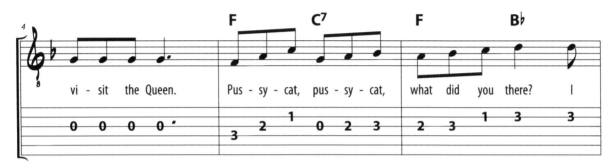

vi - sit the Queen. Pus - sy - cat, pus - sy - cat, what did you there? I

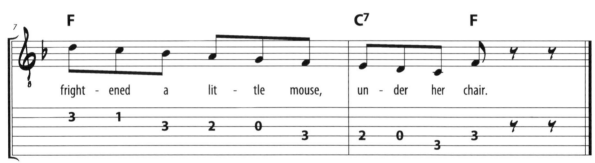

fright - ened a lit - tle mouse, un - der her chair.

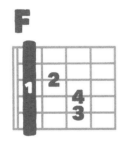

F

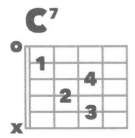

C⁷

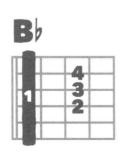

B♭

Ride a cock-horse

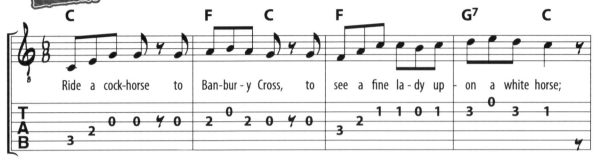

Ride a cock-horse to Ban-bur-y Cross, to see a fine la-dy up - on a white horse;

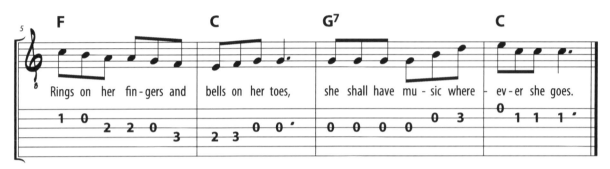

Rings on her fin-gers and bells on her toes, she shall have mu - sic where - ev - er she goes.

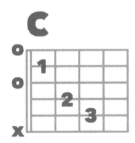

C

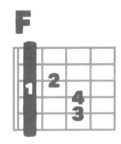

F

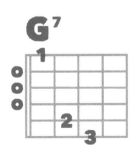

G⁷

o market, to market

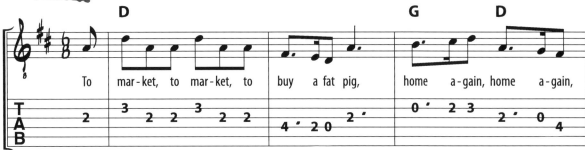

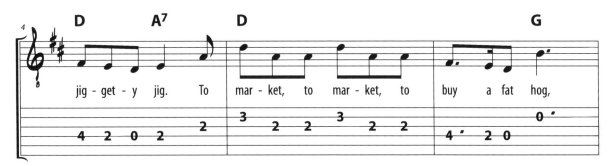

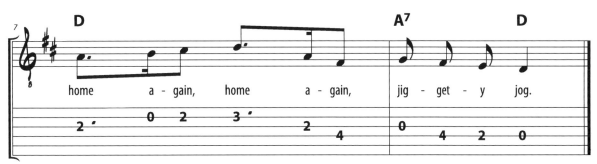

2. To market, to market, to buy a fat hog,
   Home again, home again, jiggety-jog.

3. To market, to market, to buy a plum bun,
   Home again, home again, market is done.

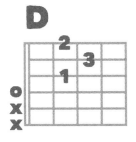

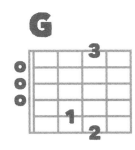

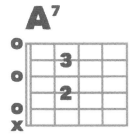

Three blind mice

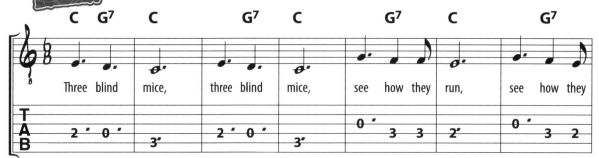

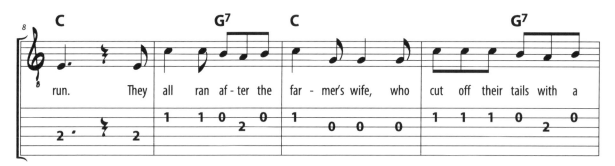

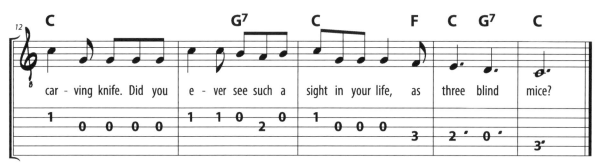

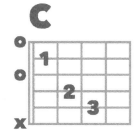

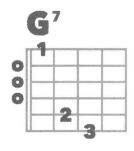

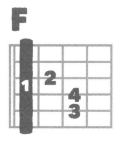

The muffin man

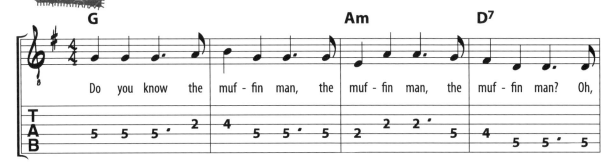

Do you know the muf-fin man, the muf-fin man, the muf-fin man? Oh,

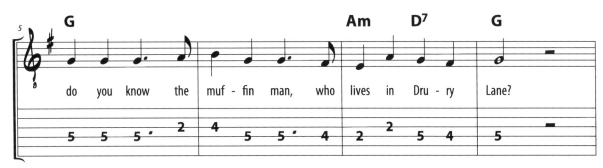

do you know the muf-fin man, who lives in Dru-ry Lane?

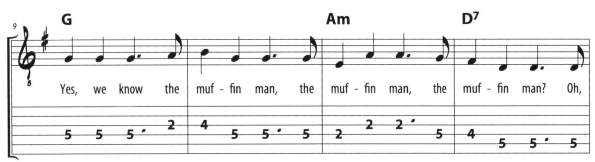

Yes, we know the muf-fin man, the muf-fin man, the muf-fin man? Oh,

yes we know the muf-fin man, who lives in Dru-ry Lane.

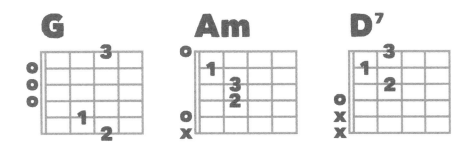

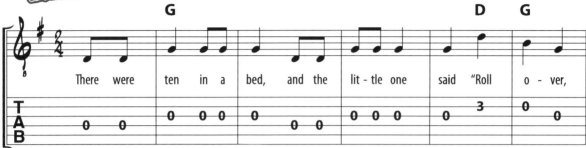

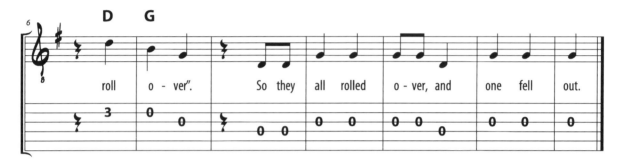

2. There were nine in a bed …

3. There were eight in a bed …

4. There were seven in a bed …

5. There were six in a bed …

6. There were five in a bed …

7. There were four in a bed …

8. There were three in a bed …

9. There were two in a bed …

10. There was one in a bed and the little one said "Good night!"

First line: hold up all ten fingers.

Second line: slowly bring hands together, indicating "small".

Third line: rotate hands over each other.

Last two lines: imitate falling out of bed with your hands.

Second verse
First line: hold up all ten fingers.

… continue down to "one"

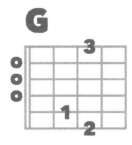

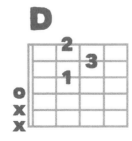

Alice the camel

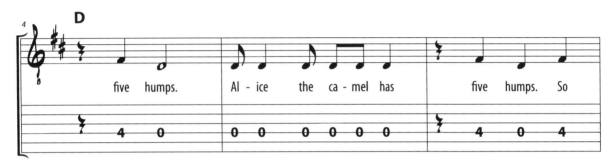

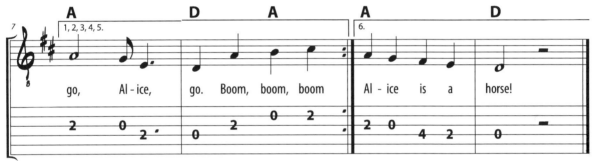

2. Alice the camel has four humps. (3x)
   So go, Alice, go.

3. Alice the camel has three humps. (3x)
   So go, Alice, go.

4. Alice the camel has two humps. (3x)
   So go, Alice, go.

5. Alice the camel has one hump. (3x)
   So go, Alice, go.

6. Alice the camel has no humps. (3x)
   Boom, Boom; Boom - Alice is a horse!

ead and shoulders, knees and toes

Head   and shoul-ders, knees and | toes, knees and toes. | Head   and shoul-ders, knees and

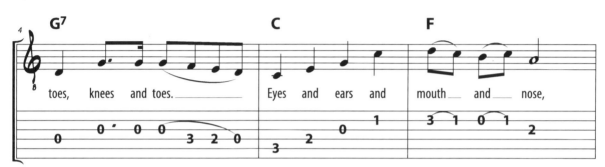

toes,   knees   and toes. | Eyes and ears and | mouth and nose,

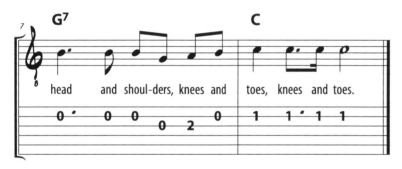

head   and shoul-ders, knees and | toes, knees and toes.

2. *Feet and tummies arms and chins, arms and chins.*
   Feet and tummies arms and chins, arms and chins.
   Eyes and ears and mouth and shins,
   feet and tummies arms and chins, arms and chins.

3. *Hands and fingers legs and lips, legs and lips.*
   Hands and fingers legs and lips, legs and lips.
   Eyes and ears and mouth and hips,
   hands and fingers legs and lips, legs and lips.

The children touch the different parts of the body when singing about them. Variant: the children repeat the song, omitting the word "head", but still touching their heads. Repeat, leaving out "head and shoulders". Keep on omitting until you do all actions silently.

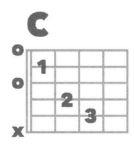

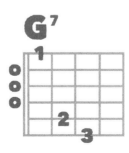

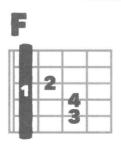

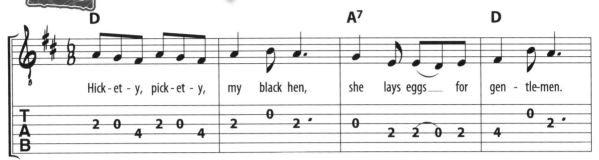

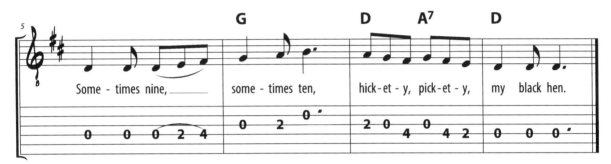

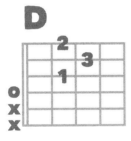

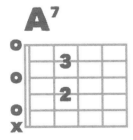

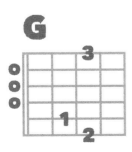

If all the world were paper

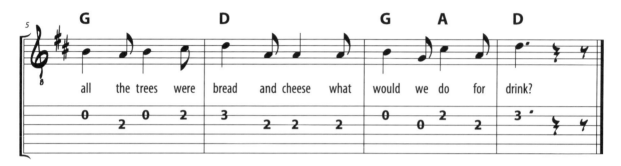

2. If all the world were sand-o,
   oh then what should we lack-o,
   if as they say there were no clay
   how should we take Tobacco?

3. If all our vessels ran-a,
   if none but had a crack-a,
   if Spanish apes ate all the grapes
   how should we do for sack-a?

4. If all the world were men
   and men lived all in trenches,
   and there were none but we alone,
   how should we do for wenches?

5. If friars had no bald pates,
   nor nuns had no dark cloisters,
   if all the seas were beans and peas
   how should we do for oysters?

6. If there had been no projects
   nor none that did great wrongs,
   if fiddlers shall turn players all
   how should we do for songs?

7. If all things were eternal
   and nothing their end bringing,
   if this should be, then how should we
   here make an end of singing?

This comic poem appears in John Mennes and James Smiths "Facetiae", probably published in 1658. Today, mostly the first verse is sung as a children's song.

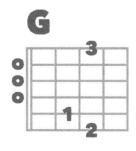
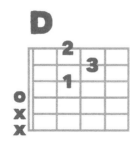
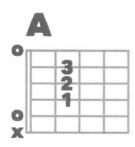

Little Bo-Peep

G   **D⁷**   **G**   **D⁷**

Lit - tle Bo-Peep has   lost   her sheep,   and   did - n't know where___ to   find   them,

G   **D⁷**   **G**   **D⁷**   **G**

leave them a - lone,   and   they'll   come home,   wag - ging their tails___ be - hind them.

2. Little Bo-Peep fell fast asleep,
   and dreamt she heard them bleating,
   but when she awoke, she found it a joke,
   for they were still a-fleeting.

3. Then up she took her little crook,
   determined for to find them,
   she found them indeed, but it made her heart bleed,
   for they'd left their tails behind them.

4. It happened one day, as Bo-Peep did stray
   into a meadow hard by,
   there she espied their tails side by side,
   all hung on a tree to dry.

5. She heaved a sigh and wiped her eye,
   and over the hillocks went rambling,
   and tried what she could, as a shepherdess should,
   to tack each again to its lambkin.

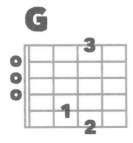

G

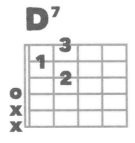

D⁷

Little boy blue

Lit - tle boy blue, come blow___ your horn, the sheep's in the mead - ow, the

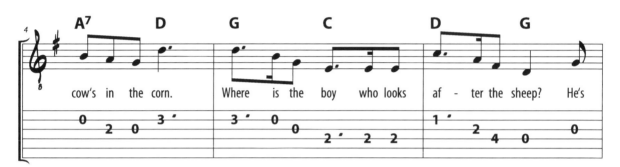

cow's in the corn. Where is the boy who looks af - ter the sheep? He's

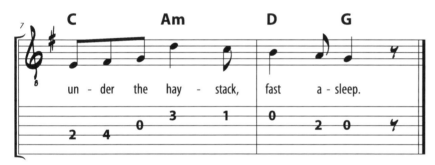

un - der the hay - stack, fast a - sleep.

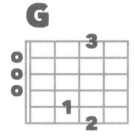

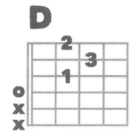

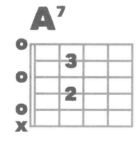

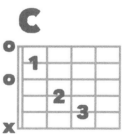

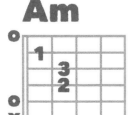

Little Tommy Tucker

Lit - tle Tom-my Tuck - er   sings for his sup - per.   What   shall we give___ him?

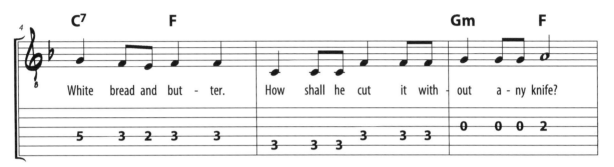

White   bread and but - ter.   How   shall he cut   it with - out   a - ny knife?

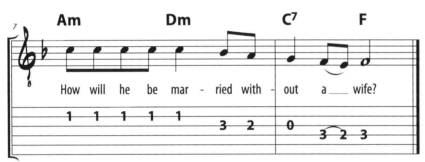

How will he   be mar - ried with - out   a ___ wife?

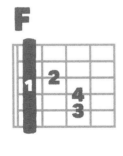
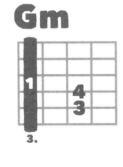
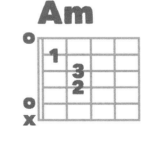
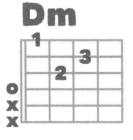

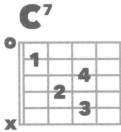

One, two, three, four, five

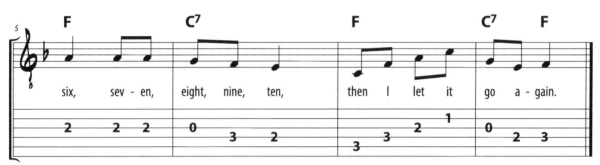

2. Why did you let it go?
   Because it bit my finger so.
   Which finger did it bite?
   This little finger on the right.

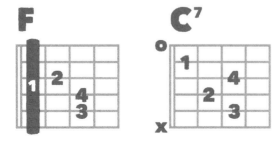

Over the river

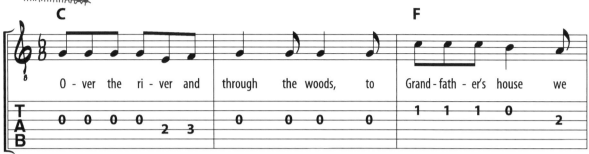

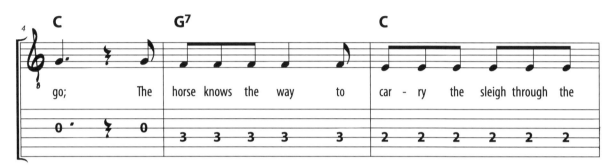

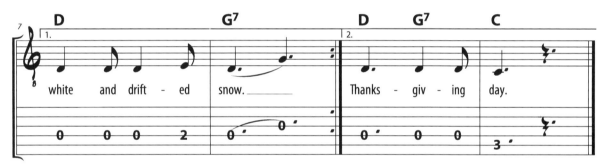

2. Over the river and through the woods,
   oh, how the wind does blow!
   It stings the toes and bites the nose,
   as over the ground we go.

3. Over the river and through the woods,
   and straight through the barnyard gate;
   We seem to go extremely slow,
   it is so hard to wait!

4. Over the river and through the woods,
   when Grandmother sees us come,
   She will say, "O, dear, the children are here,
   bring a pie for everyone."

5. Over the river and through the woods,
   now Grandmother's cap I spy!
   Hurrah for the fun! Is the pudding done?
   Hurrah for the pumpkin pie!

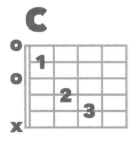
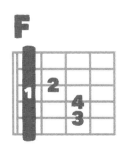
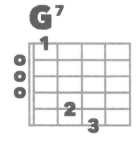
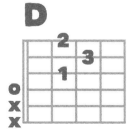

Rub-a-dub-dub

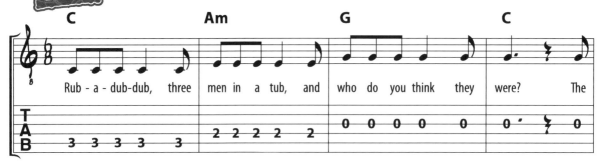

Rub - a - dub-dub, three men in a tub, and who do you think they were? The

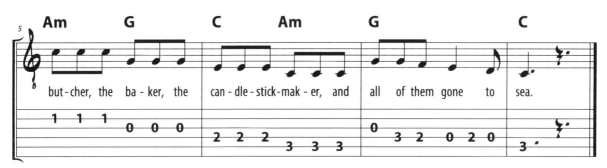

but-cher, the ba-ker, the can-dle-stick-mak-er, and all of them gone to sea.

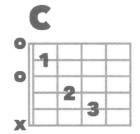

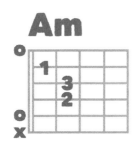

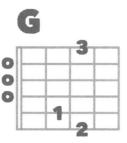

Ten green bottles

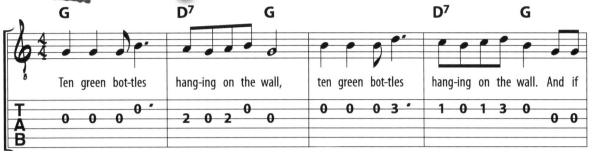

Ten green bot-tles hang-ing on the wall, ten green bot-tles hang-ing on the wall. And if

one green bot-tle should ac-ci-dent-'ly fall, there'll be nine green bot-tles hang-ing on the wall.

2.   Nine green bottles hanging on the wall …
3.   Eight green bottles hanging on the wall …
4.   Seven green bottles hanging on the wall …
5.   Six green bottles hanging on the wall …
6.   Five green bottles hanging on the wall …
7.   Four green bottles hanging on the wall …
8.   Three green bottles hanging on the wall …
9.   Two green bottles hanging on the wall …

10.   One green bottle hanging on the wall,
        one green bottle hanging on the wall.
        And if that green bottle should accidentally fall,
        there'll be no more bottles hanging on the wall.

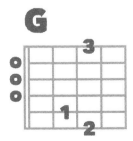
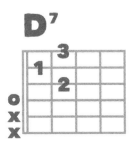
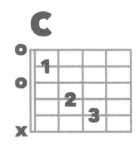
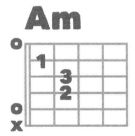

Sweetly sings the donkey

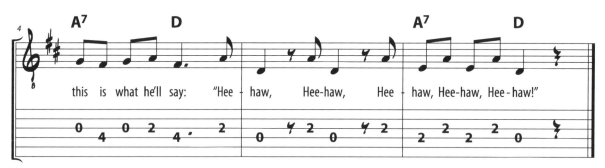

Ten little Indians

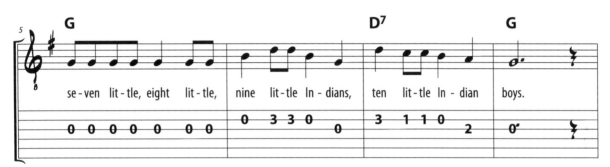

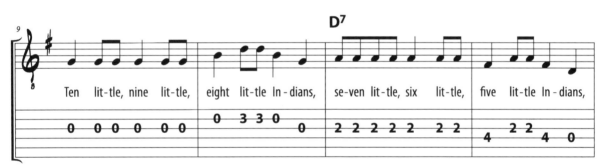

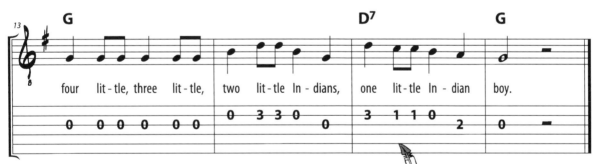

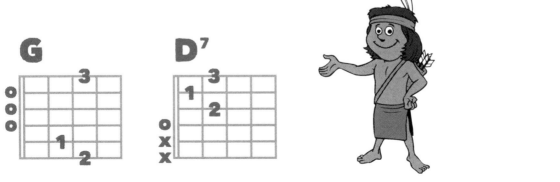

The ants go marching

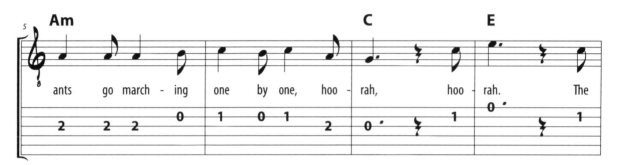

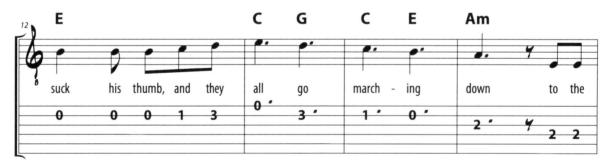

The ants go marching two by two, hoorah, hoorah,
the ants go marching two by two, hoorah, hoorah.
The ants go marching two by two,
the little one stops to tie his shoe,
and they all go marching down to the ground,
to get out of the rain. Boom! Boom! Boom!

The ants go marching three by three, hoorah, hoorah,
the ants go marching three by three, hoorah, hoorah.
The ants go marching three by three,
the little one stops to climb a tree,
and they all go marching down to the ground,
to get out of the rain. Boom! Boom! Boom!

The ants go marching four by four,hoorah, hoorah,
the ants go marching four by four, hoorah, hoorah.
The ants go marching four by four,
the little one stops to shut the door,
and they all go marching down to the ground,
to get out of the rain. Boom! Boom! Boom!

The ants go marching five by five, hurrah, hurrah,
the ants go marching five by five, hurrah, hurrah.
The ants go marching five by five,
the little one stops to take a dive
and they all go marching down to the ground
to get out of the rain. Boom! Boom! Boom!

The ants go marching six by six, hurrah, hurrah,
the ants go marching six by six, hurrah, hurrah.
The ants go marching six by six,
the little one stops to pick up sticks,
and they all go marching down to the ground,
to get out of the rain. Boom! Boom! Boom!

The ants go marching seven by seven, hurrah, hurrah,
the ants go marching seven by seven, hurrah, hurrah.
The ants go marching seven by seven,
the little one stops to pray to heaven,
and they all go marching down to the ground,
to get out of the rain. Boom! Boom! Boom!

The ants go marching eight by eight, hurrah, hurrah,
the ants go marching eight by eight, hurrah, hurrah.
The ants go marching eight by eight,
the little one stops to roller skate,
and they all go marching down to the ground,
to get out of the rain. Boom! Boom! Boom!

The ants go marching nine by nine, hurrah, hurrah,
The ants go marching nine by nine, hurrah, hurrah.
The ants go marching nine by nine,
the little one stops to check the time,
and they all go marching down to the ground,
to get out of the rain. Boom! Boom! Boom!

The ants go marching ten by ten, hurrah, hurrah,
the ants go marching ten by ten, hurrah, hurrah.
The ants go marching ten by ten,
the little one stops to shout "The End",
and they all go marching down to the ground,
to get out of the rain.

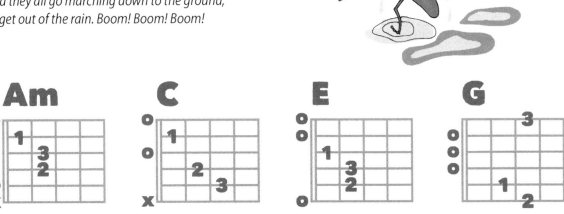

Am
C
E
G

The old gray mare

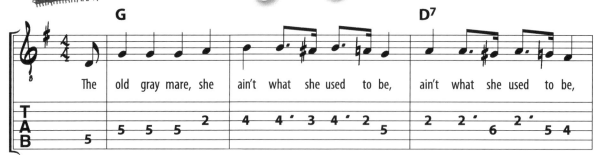

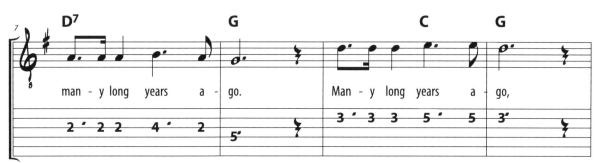

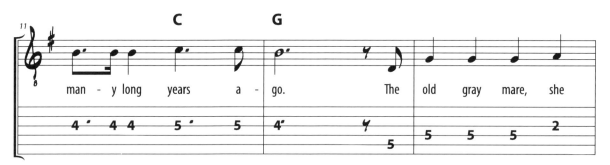

2. *The old gray mare, she kicked on the whiffletree,*
   kicked on the whiffletree, kicked on the whiffletree.
   The old gray mare, she kicked on the whiffletree,
   many long years ago.
   Many long years ago, many long years ago.
   The old gray mare, she kicked on the whiffletree,
   Many long years ago.

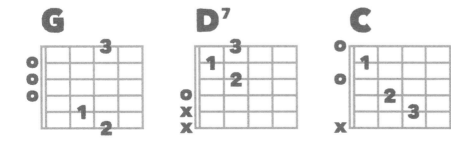

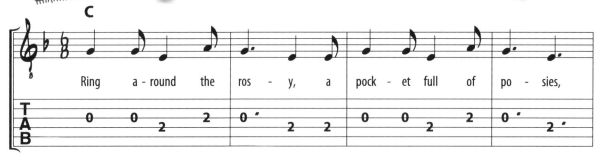

Ring a-round the ros - y, a pock - et full of po - sies,

ash - es, ash - es, we all fall down!

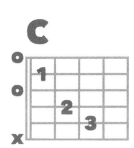

C

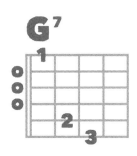

G⁷

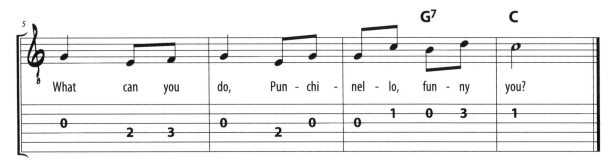

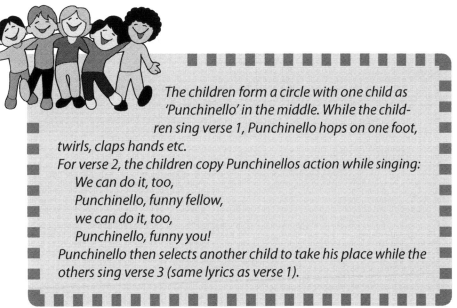

The children form a circle with one child as 'Punchinello' in the middle. While the children sing verse 1, Punchinello hops on one foot, twirls, claps hands etc.

For verse 2, the children copy Punchinellos action while singing:
  We can do it, too,
  Punchinello, funny fellow,
  we can do it, too,
  Punchinello, funny you!

Punchinello then selects another child to take his place while the others sing verse 3 (same lyrics as verse 1).

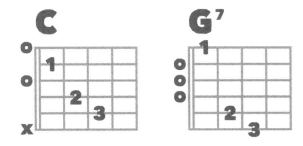

99 Bottles

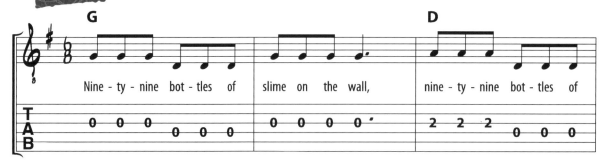

Nine - ty - nine bot - tles of slime on the wall, nine - ty - nine bot - tles of

slime; _____ and one fell down and broke its crown,

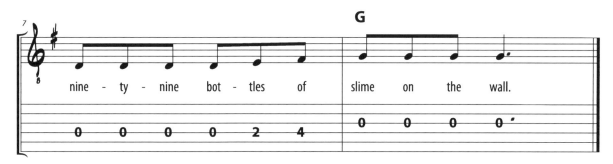

nine - ty - nine bot - tles of slime on the wall.

2. 98 bottles of slime on the wall,
   98 bottles of slime.
   One fell down and broke its crown,
   98 bottles of slime on the wall.
   etc.

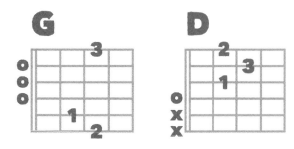

Amazing grace

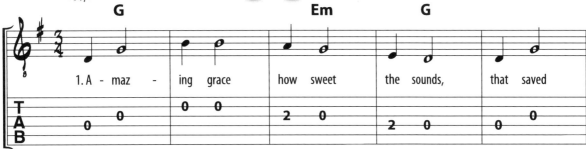

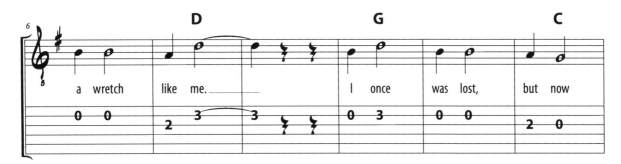

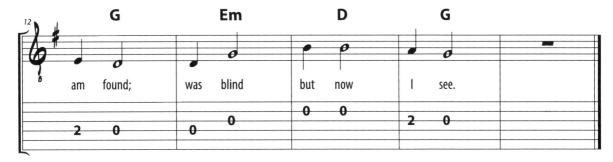

2. 'Twas grace that taught my heart to fear,
   And grace my fear relived.
   How precious did that grace appear,
   The hour I first believed.

3. When we've been there ten thousand years,
   Bright shining as the sun.
   We've no less days to sing God's praise,
   Than when we first begun.

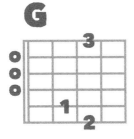
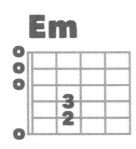
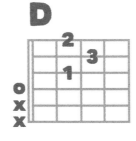
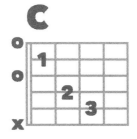

-tisket, a-tasket

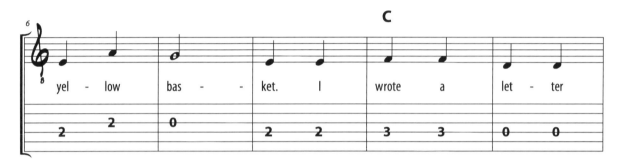

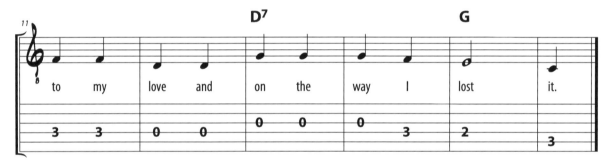

1. A-tisket a-tasket,
   a green and yellow basket,
   I wrote a letter to my love
   and on the way I lost it.

G 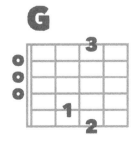   **C** 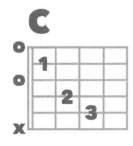   **D⁷**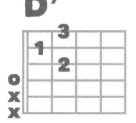

Hush, little baby

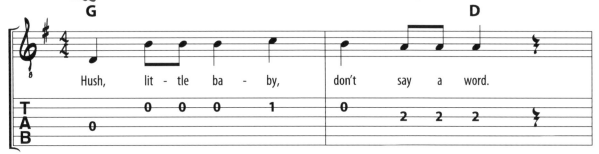

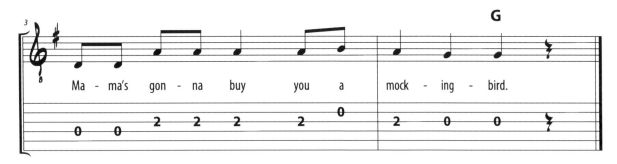

2. If that mockingbird won't sing,
   mama's gonna buy you a diamond ring.

3. If that diamond ring turns brass,
   mama's gonna buy you a looking glass.

4. If that looking glass gets broke,
   mama's gonna buy you a billy goat.

5. If that billy goat don't pull,
   mama's gonna buy you a cart and bull.

6. If that cart and bull turn over,
   mama's gonna buy you a dog named Rover.

7. If that dog named Rover won't bark,
   mama's gonna buy you a horse and cart.

8. If that horse and cart fall down,
   you'll be the sweetest little baby in town.

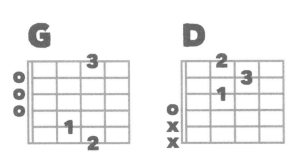

Pop goes the weasel

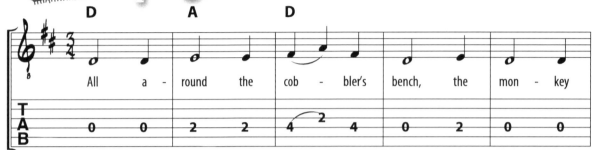

All a - round the cob - bler's bench, the mon - key

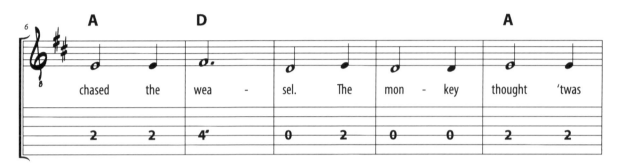

chased the wea - sel. The mon - key thought 'twas

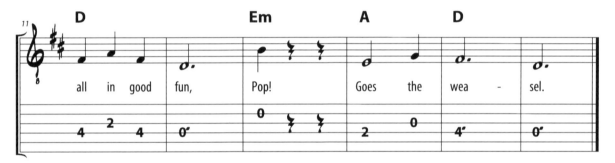

all in good fun, Pop! Goes the wea - sel.

2. A penny for a spool of thread,
   a penny for a needle.
   That's the way the money goes,
   Pop! Goes the weasel.

3. Jimmy's got the whooping cough
   and Timmy's got the measles.
   That's the way the story goes
   Pop! Goes the weasel.

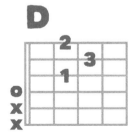

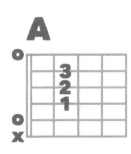

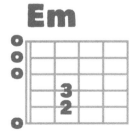

London Bridge is falling down

Lon - don bridge is | fall - ing down, | fall - ing down, | fall - ing down.

Lon - don bridge is | fall - ing down, | my fair | la - dy.

2. Take a key and lock her up,
   lock her up, lock her up.
   Take a key and lock her up,
   my fair lady.

3. How will we build it up,
   build it up, build it up?
   How will we build it up,
   my fair lady.

4. Build it up with gold and silver,
   gold and silver, gold and silver.
   Build it up with gold and silver,
   my fair lady.

5. Gold and silver I have none,
   I have none, I have none.
   Gold and silver I have none,
   my fair lady.

6. Build it up with needles and pins,
   needles and pins, needles and pins.
   Build it up with needles and pins,
   my fair lady.

7. Pins and needles bend and break,
   bend and break, bend and break.
   Pins and needles bend and break,
   my fair lady.

8. Build it up with wood and clay,
   wood and clay, wood and clay.
   Build it up with wood and clay,
   my fair lady.

9. Wood and clay will wash away,
   wash away, wash away.
   Wood and clay will wash away,
   my fair lady.

10. Build it up with stone so strong,
    stone so strong, stone so strong.
    Build it up with stone so strong,
    my fair lady.

11. Stone so strong will last so long,
    last so long, last so long.
    Stone so strong will last so long,
    my fair lady.

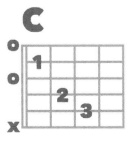

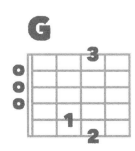

One elephant went out

One el-e-phant went out to play u – pon a spi – der's___

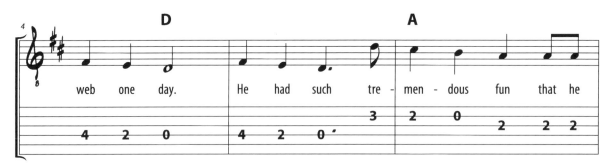

web one day. He had such tre – men – dous fun that he

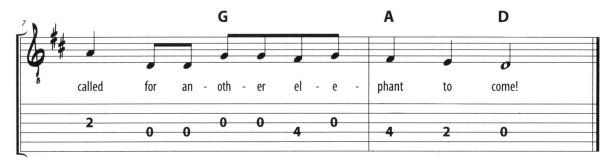

called for an – oth – er el – e – phant to come!

2. *Two Elephants went out to play upon a spider's web one day.*
   They had such tremendous fun that they called for another Elephant to come!

3. *Three Elephants went out to play upon a spider's web one day.*
   They had such tremendous fun that they called for another Elephant to come!

4. *Four Elephants went out to play upon a spider's web one day.*
   They had such tremendous fun that they called for another Elephant to come!

5. *Five Elephants went out to play upon a spider's web one day.*
   They had such tremendous fun that they all had a picnic in the sun!

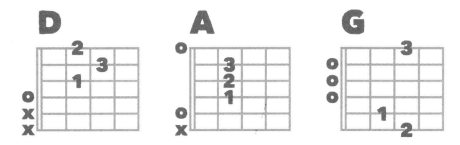

ain, rain go away

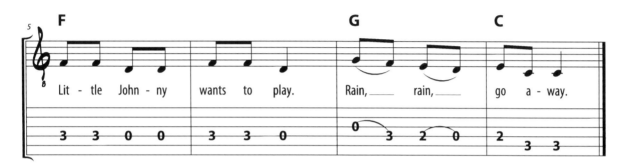

2. Rain, rain, go away,
   Come again another day.
   DADDY wants to play.
   Rain, rain, go away

3. Rain, rain, go away,
   Come again another day.
   MOMMY wants to play.
   Rain, rain, go away.

5. Rain, rain, go away,
   Come again another day.
   BROTHER wants to play.
   Rain, rain, go away.

6. Rain, rain, go away,
   Come again another day.
   SISTER wants to play.
   Rain, rain, go away.

7. Rain, rain, go away,
   Come again another day.
   BABY wants to play.
   Rain, rain, go away.

8. Rain, Rain, go away,
   Come again another day.
   ALL THE FAMILY wants to play.
   Rain, rain, go away.

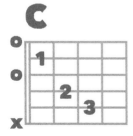 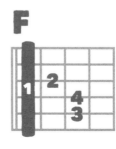 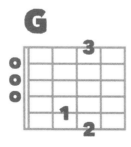

Polly wolly doodle

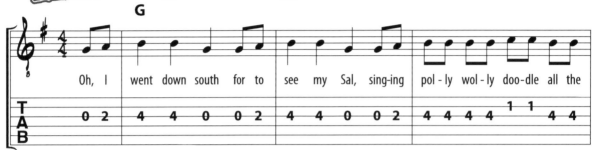

2. Oh, my Sal, she is a maiden fair,
   singing Polly wolly doodle all the day.
   With curly eyes and laughing hair,
   singing Polly wolly doodle all the day.
   Fare thee well ...

3. Behind the barn, down on my knees,
   singing Polly wolly doodle all the day.
   I thought I heard a chicken sneeze,
   singing Polly wolly doodle all the day.
   Fare thee well ...

4. He sneezed so hard with the whooping cough,
   singing Polly wolly doodle all the day.,
   He sneezed his head and the tail right off,
   singing Polly wolly doodle all the day.
   Fare thee well...

5. Oh, a grasshopper sittin' on a railroad track,
   singing Polly wolly doodle all the day.
   A-pickin' his teeth with a carpet tack,
   singing Polly wolly doodle all the day
   Fare thee well ...

6. Oh, I went to bed but it wasn't any use,
   singing Polly wolly doodle all the day.
   My feet stuck out like a chicken roost,
   singing Polly wolly doodle all the day
   Fare thee well ...

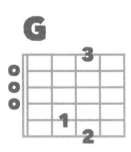

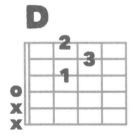

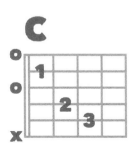

Lavender's blue

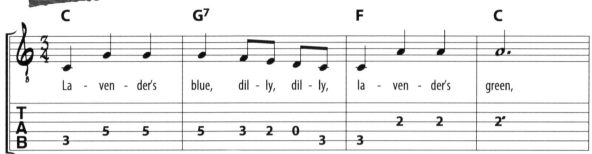

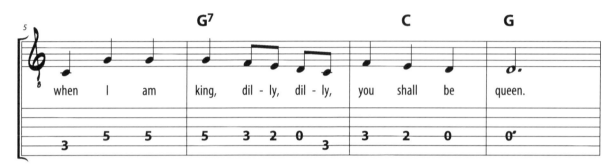

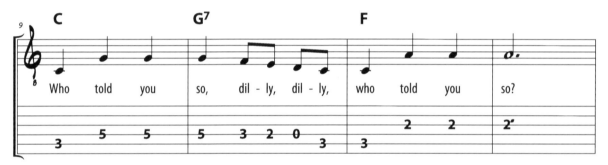

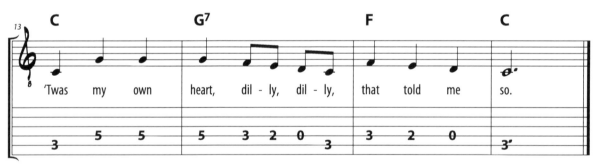

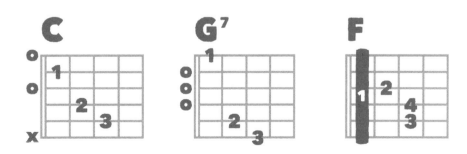

2. *Call up your men, dilly, dilly, set them to work,*
   some to the plough, dilly, dilly, some to the fork,
   some to make hay, dilly, dilly, some to cut corn,
   while you and I, dilly, dilly, keep ourselves warm.

3. *Lavender's green, dilly, dilly, Lavender's blue,*
   if you love me, dilly, dilly, I will love you.
   Let the birds sing, dilly, dilly, and the lambs play;
   we shall be safe, dilly, dilly, out of harm's way.

4. *I love to dance, dilly, dilly, I love to sing;*
   when I am queen, dilly, dilly, you'll be my king.
   Who told me so, dilly, dilly, who told me so?
   I told myself, dilly, dilly, I told me so.

Hickory dickory dock

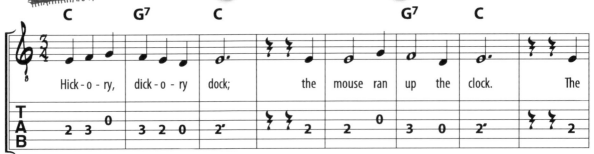

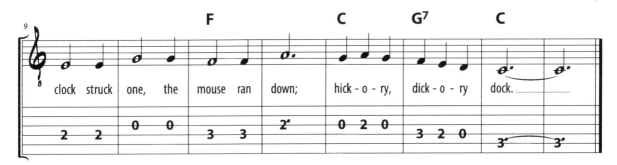

2. Hickory dickory dock,
   the mouse ran up the clock,
   the clock struck two
   and down he flew,
   hickory dickory dock.

3. Hickory dickory dock,
   the mouse ran up the clock,
   the clock struck three
   and he did flee,
   hickory dickory dock.

4. Hickory dickory dock,
   the mouse ran up the clock,
   the clock struck four,
   he hit the floor,
   hickory dickory dock.

5. Hickory dickory dock,
   the mouse ran up the clock,
   the clock struck five,
   the mouse took a dive,
   hickory dickory dock.

6. Hickory dickory dock,
   the mouse ran up the clock,
   the clock struck six,
   the mouse, he split,
   hickory dickory dock.

7. Hickory dickory dock,
   the mouse ran up the clock,
   the clock struck seven,
   8, 9, 10, 11,
   hickory dickory dock.

8. Hickory dickory dock,
   the mouse ran up the clock,
   as twelve bells rang,
   the mousie sprang,
   hickory dickory dock.

9. Hickory dickory dock,
   "Why scamper?" asked the clock,
   "You scare me so
   I have to go!"
   hickory dickory dock.

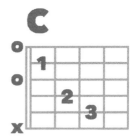

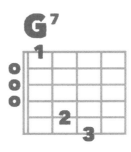

Teddy bear

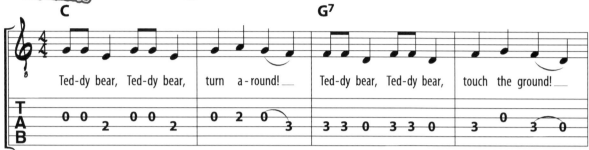

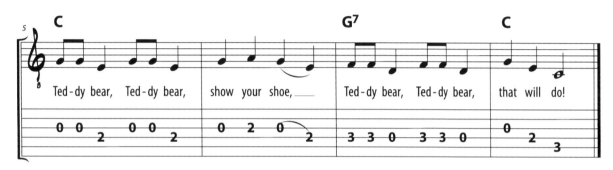

2. Teddy bear, teddy bear, turn around!
   Teddy bear, teddy bear, touch the ground!
   Teddy bear, teddy bear, jump up high!
   Teddy bear, teddy bear, touch the sky!

3. Teddy bear, teddy bear, bend down low!
   Teddy bear, teddy bear, touch you toes!
   Teddy bear, teddy bear, turn out the light!
   Teddy bear, teddy bear, say good night!

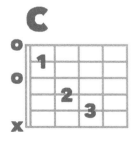

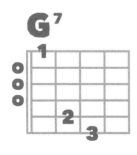

Rock-a-bye, baby

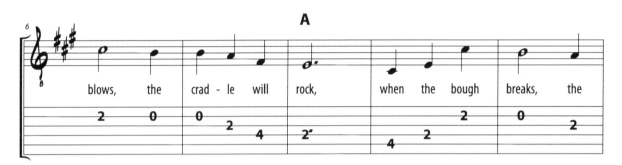

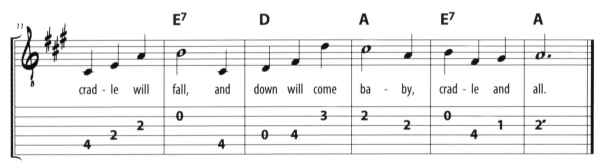

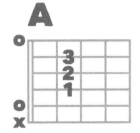

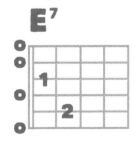

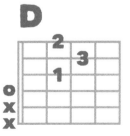

Itsy-bitsy spider

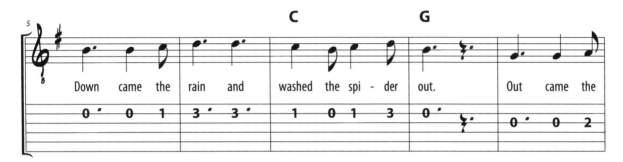

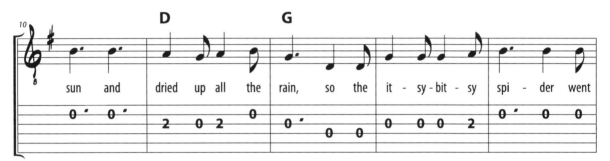

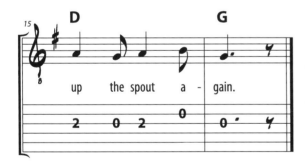

2. The great big spider went up the water spout ...

3. The teeny tiny spider went up the water spout ...

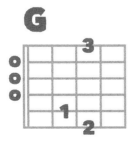
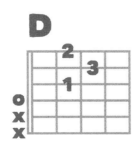
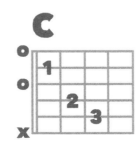

Crawdad Song

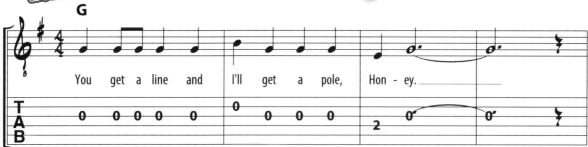

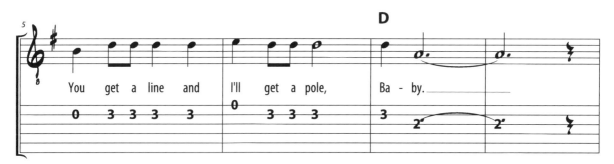

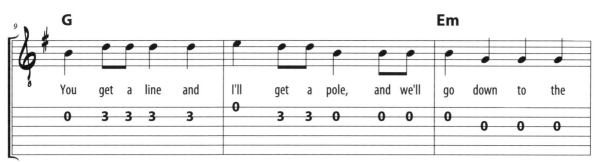

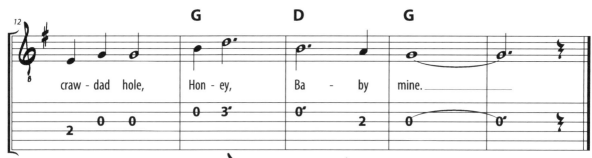

2. *Sittin' on the bank 'til my feet get cold, Honey.*
   Sittin' on the bank 'til my feet get cold, Baby.
   Sittin' on the bank 'til my feet get cold,
   lookin' down that crawdad hole, Honey, Baby mine.

3. *Yonder comes a man with a sack on his back, Honey.*
   Yonder comes a man with a sack on his Baby.
   Yonder comes a man with a sack on his back,
   packin' all the crawdads he can pack, Honey, Baby mine.

4. *The man fell down and he broke that sack, Honey.*
   The man fell down and he broke that sack, Baby.
   The man fell down and he broke that sack,
   see those crawdads backing back, Honey, Baby mine.

5. *I heard the duck say to the drake, honey, honey.*
   I heard the duck say to the drake, baby, baby.
   I heard the duck say to the drake,
   there ain't no crawdads in this lake, Honey, Baby mine.

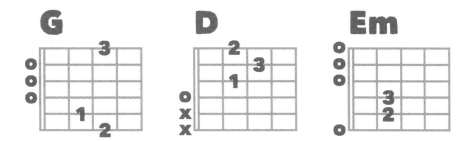

Baa, baa, black sheep

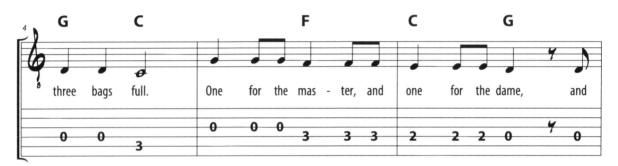

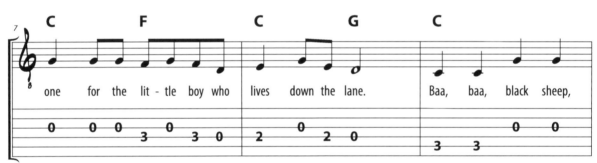

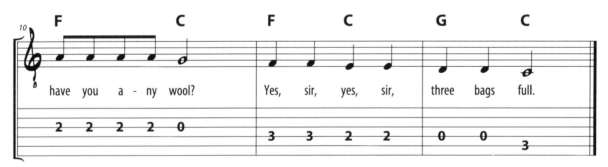

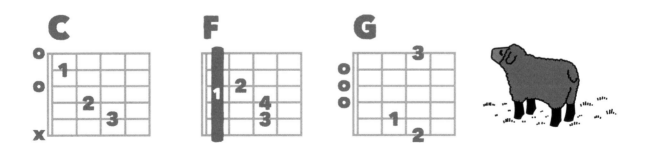

Bingo

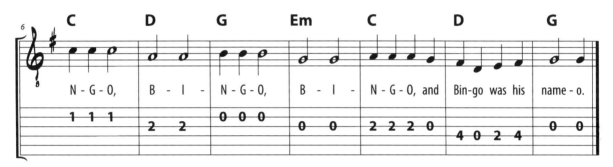

2. There was a man who had a dog,
   and Bingo was his name-o.
   (clap)-I-N-G-O (3x)
   and Bingo was his name-o.

3. There was a man who had a dog,
   and Bingo was his name-o.
   (clap)-(clap)-N-G-O (3x)
   and Bingo was his name-o.

4. There was a man who had a dog,
   and Bingo was his name-o.
   (clap)-(clap)-(clap)-G-O (3x)
   and Bingo was his name-o.

5. There was a man who had a dog,
   and Bingo was his name-o.
   (clap)-(clap)-(clap)-(clap)-O (3x)
   and Bingo was his name-o.

6. There was a man who had a dog,
   and Bingo was his name-o.
   (clap)-(clap)-(clap)-(clap)-(clap) (3x)
   and Bingo was his name-o.

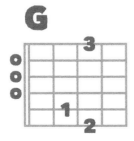
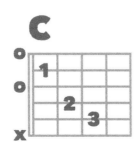
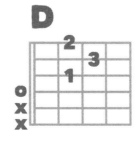
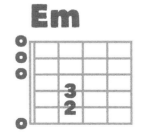

Brahms' Lullaby

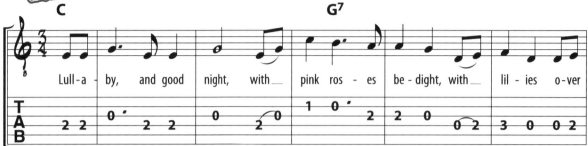

Lull-a - by, and good night, with pink ros - es be-dight, with lil - ies o-ver

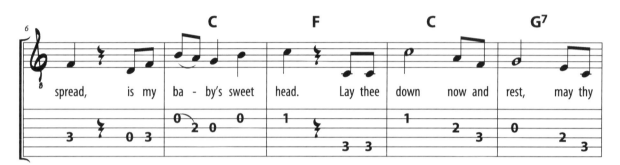

spread, is my ba - by's sweet head. Lay thee down now and rest, may thy

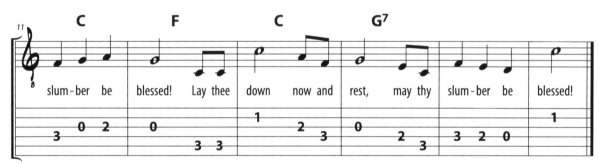

slum-ber be blessed! Lay thee down now and rest, may thy slum-ber be blessed!

2. Lullaby, and good night, your mother's delight,
shining angels beside my darling abide.
Soft and warm is your bed,
close your eyes and rest your head.
Soft and warm is your bed,
close your eyes and rest your head.

3. Sleepyhead, close your eyes,
mother's right here beside you.
I'll protect you from harm,
you will wake in my arms.
Guardian angels are near,
so sleep on, with no fear.
Guardian angels are near,
so sleep on, with no fear.

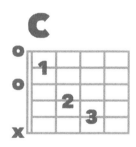

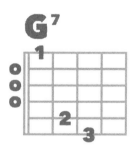

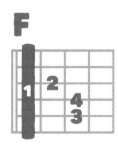

Jack and Jill

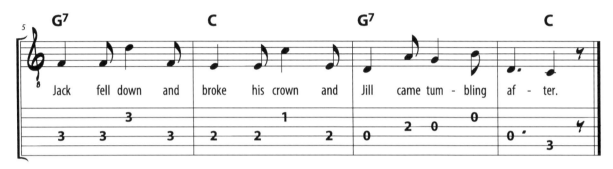

2. Up Jack got and home did trot,
   as fast as he could caper;
   and went to bed and bound his head
   with vinegar and brown paper.

3. When Jill came in how she did grin
   to see Jack's paper plaster;
   mother vexed did whip her next
   for causing Jack's disaster.

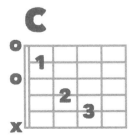
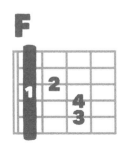
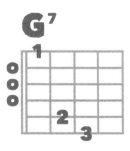

This old man

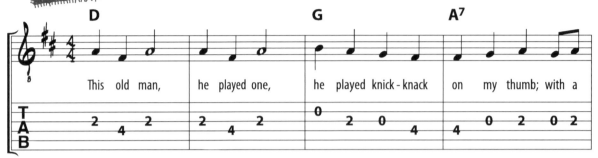

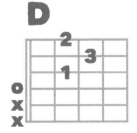

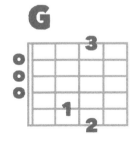

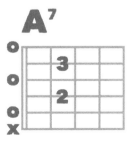

2. This old man, he played two,
   he played knick-knack on my shoe;
   with a knick-knack paddywhack,
   give the dog a bone,
   this old man came rolling home.

3. This old man, he played three,
   he played knick-knack on my knee;
   with a knick-knack paddywhack,
   give the dog a bone,
   this old man came rolling home.

4. This old man, he played four,
   he played knick-knack on my door;
   with a knick-knack paddywhack,
   give the dog a bone,
   this old man came rolling home.

5. This old man, he played five,
   he played knick-knack on my hive;
   with a knick-knack paddywhack,
   give the dog a bone,
   this old man came rolling home.

6. This old man, he played six,
   he played knick-knack on my sticks;
   with a knick-knack paddywhack,
   give the dog a bone,
   this old man came rolling home.

7. This old man, he played seven,
   he played knick-knack up in heaven;
   with a knick-knack paddywhack,
   give the dog a bone,
   this old man came rolling home.

8. This old man, he played eight,
   he played knick-knack on my gate;
   with a knick-knack paddywhack,
   give the dog a bone,
   this old man came rolling home.

9. This old man, he played nine,
   he played knick-knack on my spine;
   with a knick-knack paddywhack,
   give the dog a bone,
   this old man came rolling home.

10. This old man, he played ten,
    he played knick-knack once again;
    with a knick-knack paddywhack,
    give the dog a bone,
    this old man came rolling home.

J. J. Schmidt

John   Ja - cob   Jin - gle - hei - mer Schmidt,   his   name is my   name,

too.   When - ev - er   we   go   out,   the   peo - ple   al - ways shout:

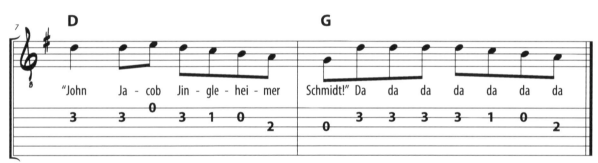

"John   Ja - cob   Jin - gle - hei - mer   Schmidt!" Da   da   da   da   da   da   da

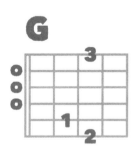

G

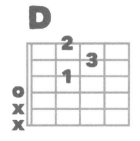

D

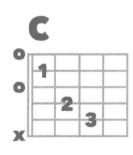

C

Little green frog

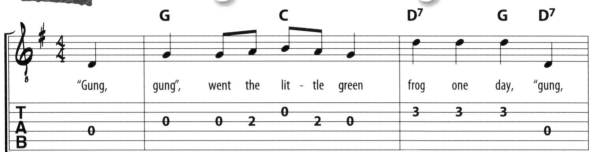

"Gung, gung", went the lit - tle green frog one day, "gung,

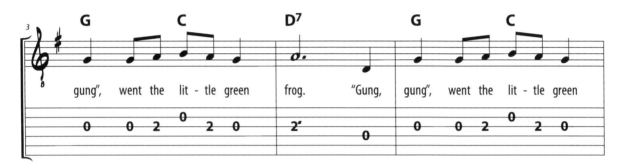

gung", went the lit - tle green frog. "Gung, gung", went the lit - tle green

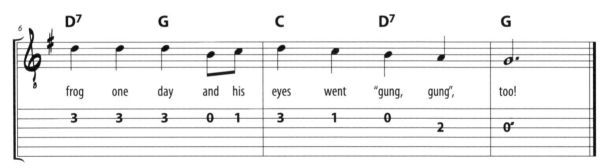

frog one day and his eyes went "gung, gung", too!

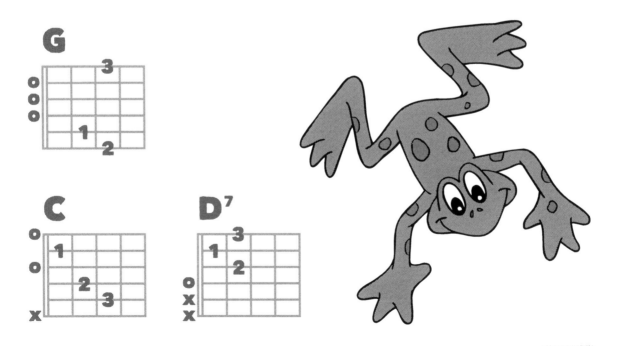

G

C   D⁷

Camptown races

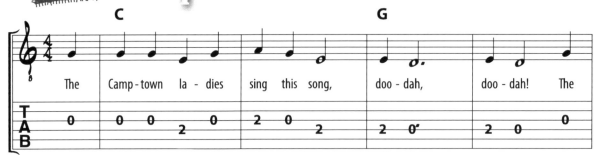

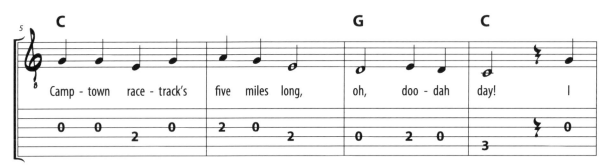

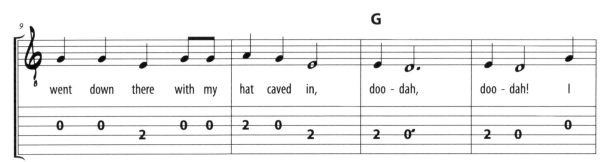

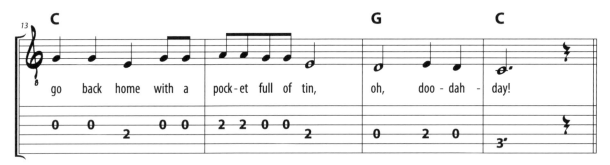

2. De long tail filly and de big black hoss, Doo-dah! doo-dah!
   Dey fly de track and dey both cut across, Oh, doo-dah-day!
   De blind hoss sticken in a big mud hole, Doo-dah! doo-dah!
   Can't touch bottom wid a ten foot pole, Oh, doo-dah-day

Refrain

3. Old muley cow come on to de track, Doo-dah! doo-dah!
   De bob-tail fling her ober his back, Oh, doo-dah-day!
   Den fly along like a rail-road car, Doo-dah! doo-dah!
   Runnin' a race wid a shootin' star, Oh, doo-dah-day!

Refrain

4. See dem flyin' on a ten mile heat, Doo-dah doo-dah!
   Round de race track, den repeat, Oh, doo-dah-day!
   I win my money on de bob-tail nag, Doo-dah! doo-dah!
   I keep my money in an old tow-bag, Oh, doo-dah-day!

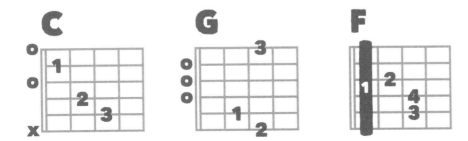

Marianne

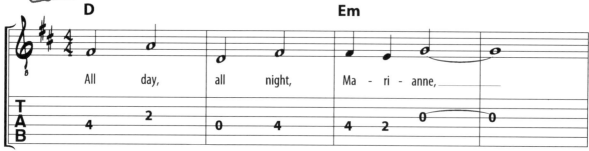

D   Em

All   day,   all   night,   Ma - ri - anne,

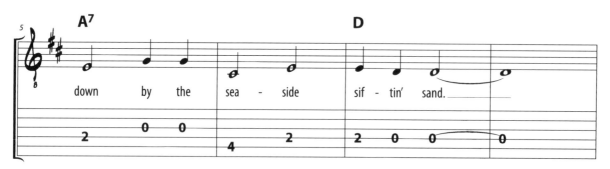

A⁷   D

down   by   the   sea - side   sif - tin' sand.

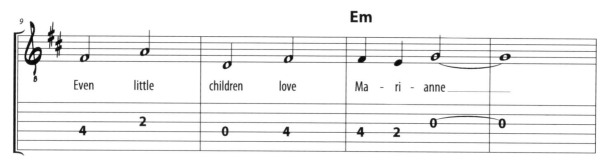

Em

Even   little   children   love   Ma - ri - anne

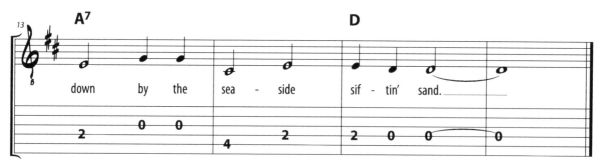

A⁷   D

down   by   the   sea - side   sif - tin' sand.

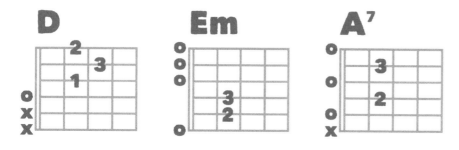

Good morn - ing, good morn - ing, and how do you do? Good

morn - ing, good morn - ing, I'm fine, how are you?

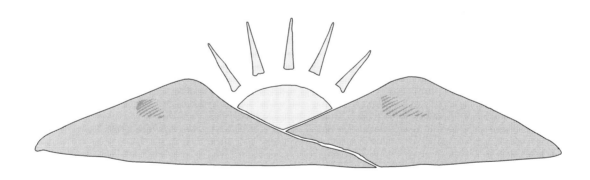

D

G

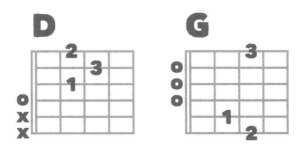

If you're happy

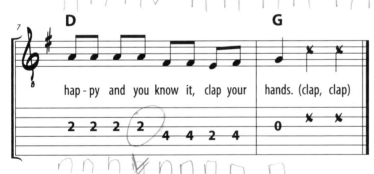

2. ... stomp your feet (stomp, stomp)

3. ... slap your legs (slap slap)

4. ... slap your knees (slap slap)

5. ... nod your head (nod nod)

6. ... tap your toe (tap tap)

7. ... honk your nose (honk honk)

etc.

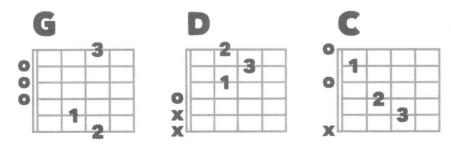

Hey, diddle, diddle

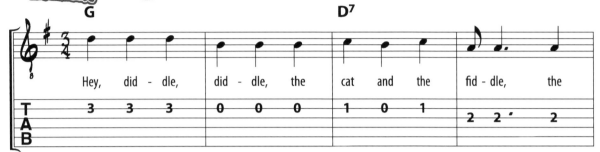

Hey, did - dle, did - dle, the cat and the fid - dle, the

cow jumped o - ver the moon; the

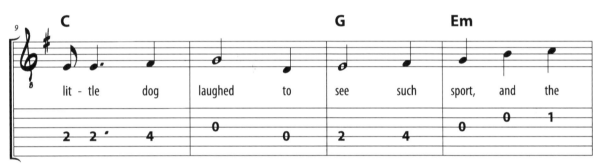

lit - tle dog laughed to see such sport, and the

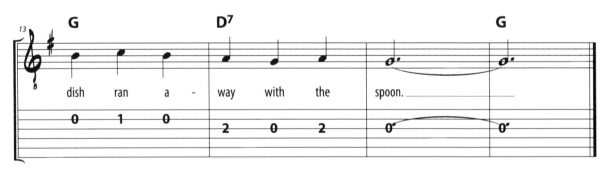

dish ran a - way with the spoon.

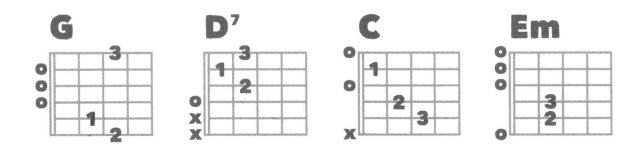

G D⁷ C Em

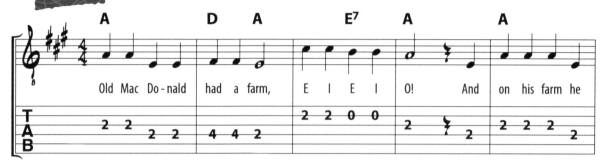

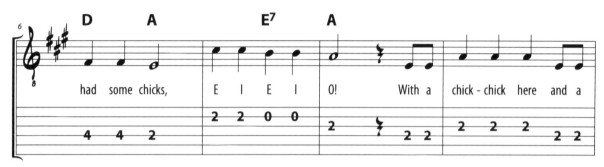

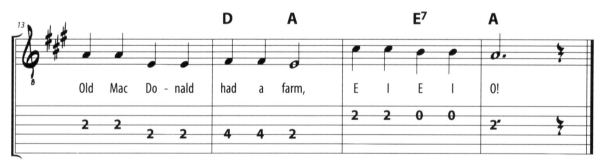

2. ... he had some geese ...
   With a gabble-gabble here ...
3. ... he had a pig ...
   With an oinck-oink here ...
4. ... he had some ducks ...
   With a quack-quack here ...
5. ... he had a cow ...
   With a moo-moo here ...

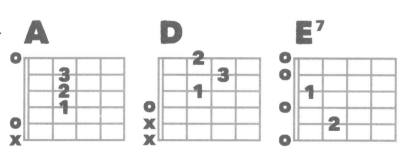

Sleep, baby, sleep

2. Sleep, baby, sleep.
   Your father guards the sheep.
   Your mother shakes the dreamland tree,
   down falls a little dream for thee,
   Sleep, baby, sleep.

3. Sleep, baby, sleep.
   Your father watches the sheep.
   The wind is blowing fierce and wild,
   it must not wake my little child.
   Sleep, baby, sleep.

4. Sleep, baby sleep.
   The large stars are the sheep.
   The little stars are the lambs, I guess,
   the gentle moon's the shepherdess.
   Sleep, baby, sleep.

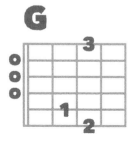

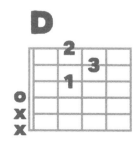

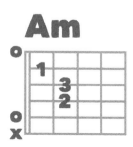

There's a hole in the bucket

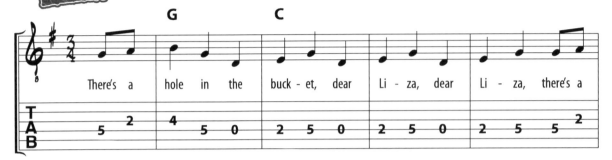

There's a hole in the buck-et, dear Li-za, dear Li-za, there's a

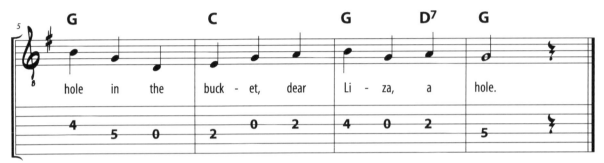

hole in the buck-et, dear Li-za, a hole.

2. Then fix it, dear Henry, dear Henry, dear Henry,
    then fix it, dear Henry, dear Henry, fix it.

3. With what shall I fix it, dear Liza, dear Liza?
    with what shall I fix it, dear Liza, with what?

4. With straw, dear Henry, dear Henry, dear Henry,
    With straw, dear Henry, dear Henry, with straw.

5. The straw is too long, dear Liza, dear Liza,
    the straw is too long, dear Liza, too long.

6. Then cut it, dear Henry, dear Henry, dear Henry,
    then cut it, dear Henry, dear Henry, cut it.

7. With what shall I cut it, dear Liza, dear Liza?
    With what shall I cut it, dear Liza, with what?

8. With a knife, dear Henry, dear Henry, dear Henry,
    with a knife, dear Henry, dear Henry, with a knife.

9. The knife is too dull, dear Liza, dear Liza,
    the knife is too dull, dear Liza, too dull.

10. *Then sharpen it, dear Henry, dear Henry, dear Henry,*
    then sharpen it, dear Henry, dear Henry, sharpen it.

11. *On what shall I sharpen it, dear Liza, dear Liza?*
    On what shall I sharpen it, dear Liza, on what?

12. *On a stone, dear Henry, dear Henry, dear Henry,*
    on a stone, dear Henry, dear Henry, a stone.

13. *The stone is too dry, dear Liza, dear Liza,*
    the stone is too dry, dear Liza, too dry.

14. *Then wet it, dear Henry, dear Henry, dear Henry,*
    then wet it, dear Henry, dear Henry, wet it.

15. *With what shall I wet it, dear Liza, dear Liza?*
    With what shall I wet it, dear Liza, with what?

16. *Try water, dear Henry, dear Henry, dear Henry,*
    try water, dear Henry, dear Henry, water.

17. *In what shall I fetch it, dear Liza, dear Liza?*
    In what shall I fetch it, dear Liza, in what?

18. *In the bucket, dear Henry, dear Henry, dear Henry,*
    In the bucket, dear Henry, dear Henry, a bucket.

19. *But there's a hole in my bucket, dear Liza, dear Liza,*
    there's a hole in my bucket, dear Liza, a hole.

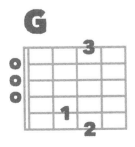

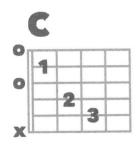

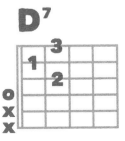

Silent night

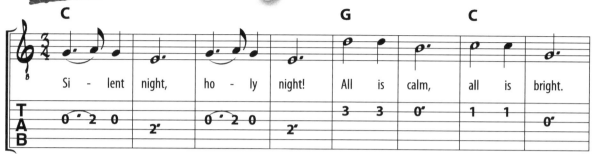

Si - lent night, ho - ly night! All is calm, all is bright.

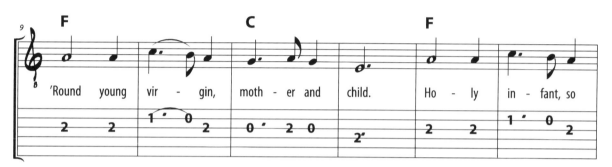

'Round young vir - gin, moth - er and child. Ho - ly in - fant, so

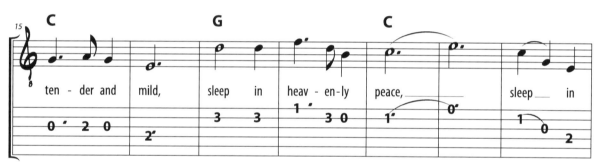

ten - der and mild, sleep in heav - en - ly peace, sleep in

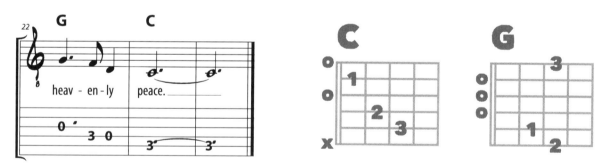

heav - en - ly peace.

2. Silent night, Holy night!
   Son of God, love's pure light.
   Radiant beams from thy holy face.
   With the dawn of redeeming grace,
   Jesus, Lord at thy birth,
   Jesus, Lord at thy birth.

3. Silent night, Holy night!
   Shepherds quake, at the sight.
   Glories stream from heaven above.
   Heavenly, hosts sing Hallelujah,
   Christ the Savior is born,
   Christ the Savior is born.

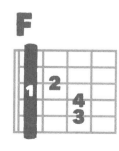

Skip to my Lou

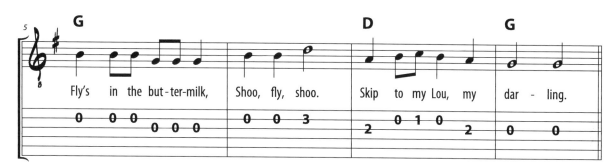

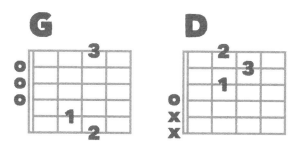

2. There's a little red wagon, Paint it blue.

3. Lost my partner, What'll I do?

4. I'll get another one, Prettier than you.

5. Can't get a red bird, Jaybird'll do.

6. Cat's in the cream jar, Ooh, ooh, ooh.

Jingle bells

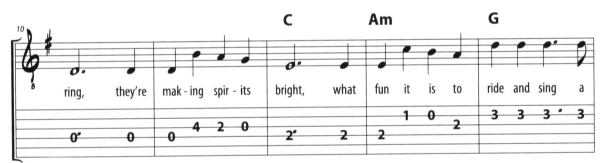

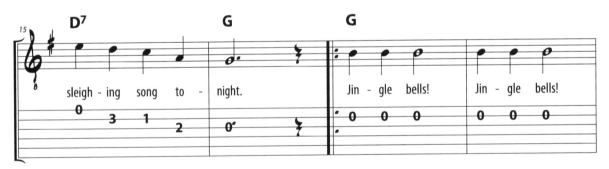

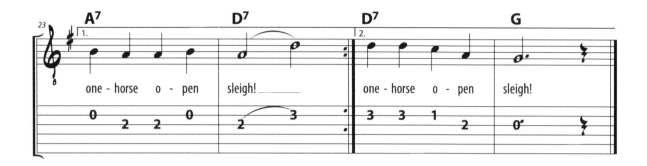

2. A day or two ago I thought I'd take a ride,
   and soon Miss Fannie Bright was seated by my side.
   The horse was lean and lank, misfortune seemed his lot,
   he got into a drifted bank and we got upsot.

3. A day or two ago, The story I must tell
   I went out on the snow, And on my back I fell;
   A gent was riding by In a one-horse open sleigh,
   he laughed as there I sprawling lie, But quickly drove away.

4. Now the ground is white, go it while you're young,
   take the girls tonight and sing this sleighing song.
   Just get a bobtailed bay, two-forty for his speed,
   then hitch him to an open sleigh, and crack! You'll take the lead.

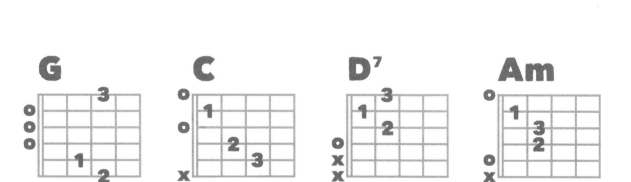

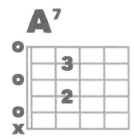

Twinkle, twinkle little Star

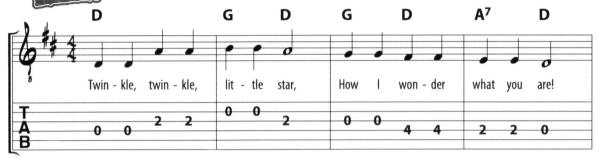

Twin - kle, twin - kle, lit - tle star, How I won - der what you are!

Up a - bove the world so high, Like a dia - mond in the sky!

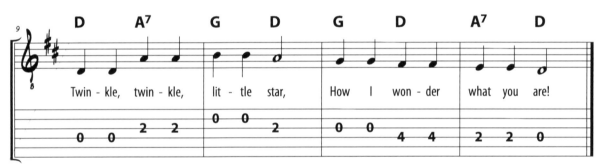

Twin - kle, twin - kle, lit - tle star, How I won - der what you are!

2. When the blazing sun is gone,
   when he nothing shines upon,
   then you show your little light,
   twinkle, twinkle, all the night.

3. Then the traveller in the dark,
   thanks you for your tiny spark,
   he could not see which way to go,
   if you did not twinkle so.

4. In the dark blue sky you keep,
   and often through my curtains peep,
   for you never shut your eye,
   till the sun is in the sky.

5. As your bright and tiny spark,
   lights the traveller in the dark,
   though I know not what you are,
   twinkle, twinkle, little star.

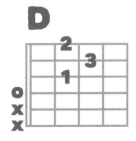
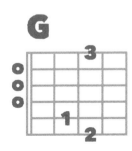
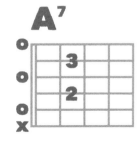
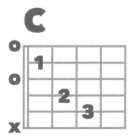

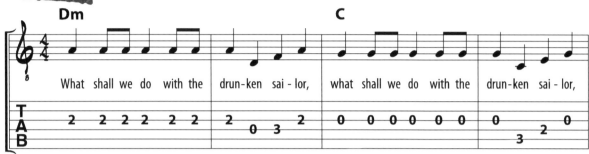

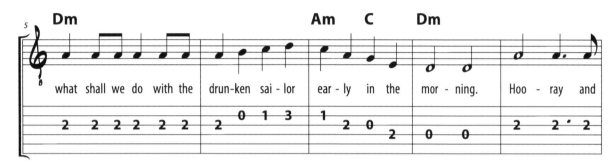

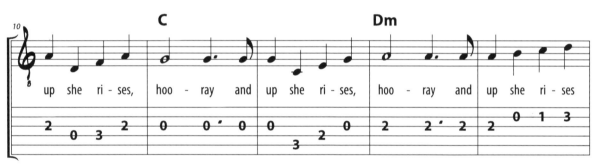

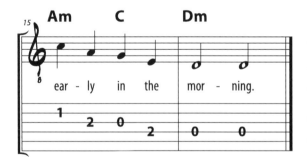

2. Give him a dose of salent water, early ...

3. Give him a dash with a besoms rubber, early ...

4. Pull out the plug and wet him all over, early ...

5. Heave him by the leg in a running bowlin', early ...

6. That's what to do with a drunken sailor, early ...

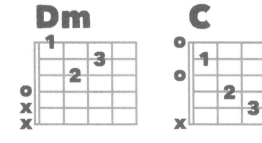

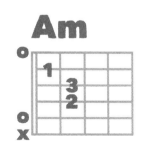

Brother John

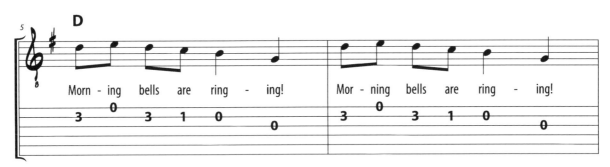

Are you sleep-ing? Are you sleep-ing? Broth-er John, Broth-er John?

Morn-ing bells are ring - ing! Mor - ning bells are ring - ing!

Ding Dang Dong, Ding Dang Dong.

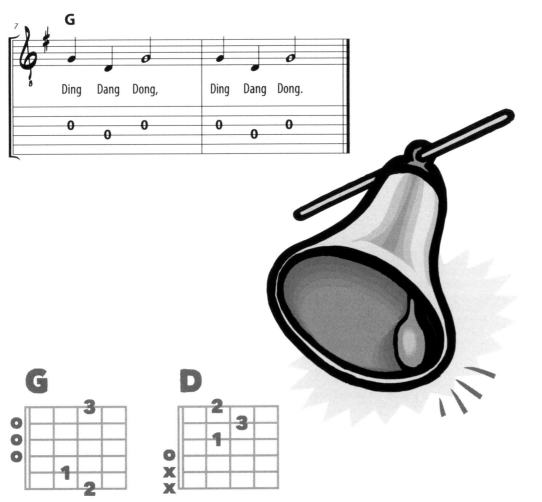

G   D

She'll be coming round the mountain

She'll be | com-in' round the | moun-tain when she | comes, _____ | She'll be

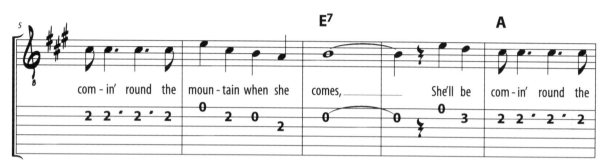

com-in' round the | moun-tain when she | comes, _____ | She'll be | com-in' round the

moun-tain, she'll be | com-in' round the | moun-tain, she'll be | com-in' round the

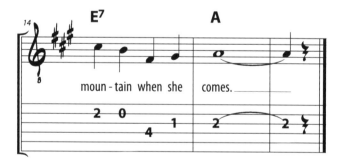

moun-tain when she | comes. _____

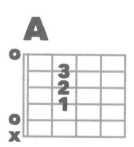

2. She'll be driving' six white horses when she comes ...
3. We will all go out to meet her when she comes ...
4. We will have chickden an' dumplin's when she comes ...
5. She'll be reelin' an' a-rockin' when she comes ...
6. We'll shout glory hallelujah when she comes ...

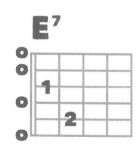

Yankee Doodle

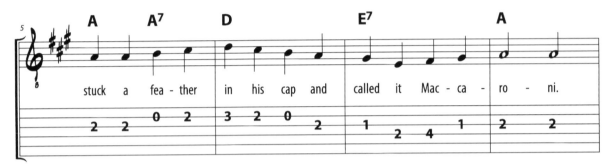

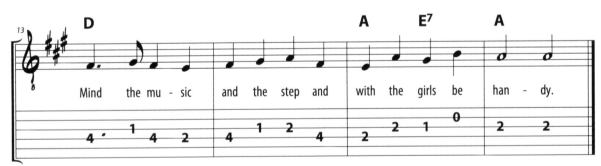

2. *Father and I went down to camp,*
   along with Captain Gooding.
   And there we saw the men and boys,
   as thick as hasty pudding.
   Yankee Doodle, keep it up,
   Yankee Doodle dandy.
   Mind the music and the step,
   and with the girls be handy.

3. *There was Captain Washington,*
   upon a slapping stallion.
   A-giving orders to his men,
   I guess there was a million.
   Yankee Doodle, keep it up,
   Yankee Doodle dandy.
   Mind the music and the step,
   and with the girls be handy.

4. *Yankee Doodle is a tune,*
   that comes in mighty handy,
   The enemies all run away,
   at Yankee Doodle Dandy!
   Yankee Doodle, keep it up,
   Yankee Doodle dandy.
   Mind the music and the step,
   and with the girls be handy.

A
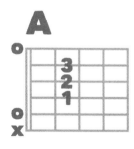

E
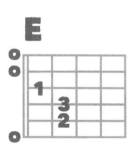

A⁷
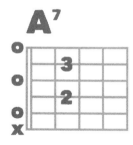

D
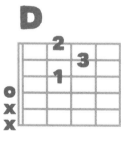

E⁷
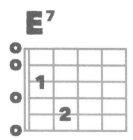

Clementine

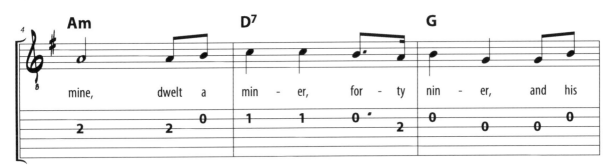

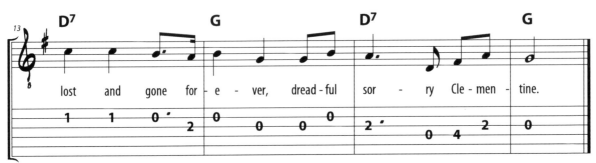

2. Light she was, and like a fairy,
   and her shoes were number nine,
   herring boxes without topses,
   sandals were for Clementine.

3. Drove she ducklings to the water
   every morning just at nine,
   struck her foot agains a splinter,
   fell into the foaming brine.

4. Rosy lips above the water,
   blowing bubbles mighty fine,
   but, alas, I was no swimmer,
   so I lost my Clementine.

5. How I missed her! How I missed her!
   How I missed my Clementine!
   But I kissed her little sister,
   and forgot my Clementine.

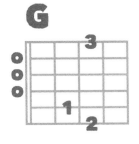
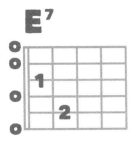
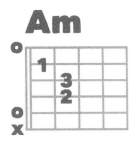
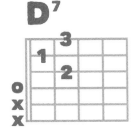

Go, tell it on the mountain

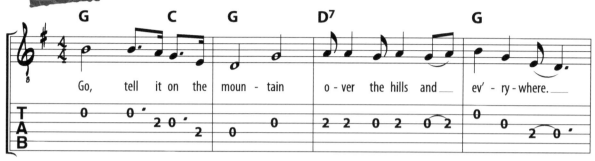

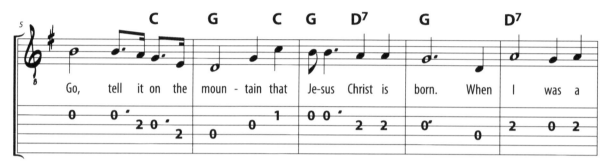

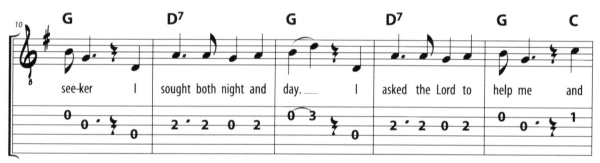

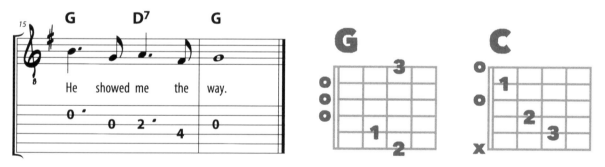

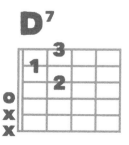

2. He made me a watchman upon the city wall,
   and if I am a christian I am the least of all.

3. 'T was a lowly manger that Jesus Christ was born.
   The Lord sent down an angel that bright and glorious morn'.

he bear went over the mountain

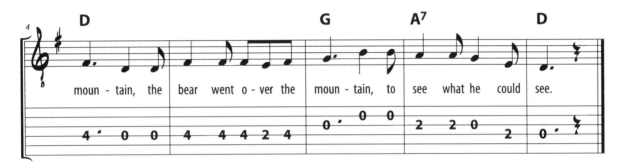

2. The other side of the mountain,
   the other side of the mountain,
   the other side of the mountain,
   was all that he could see.

3. The bear went over the river,
   the bear went over the river,
   the bear went over the river,
   to see what he could see.

4. The other side of the river,
   the other side of the river,
   the other side of the river,
   was all that he could see.

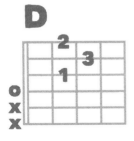

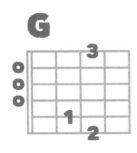

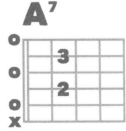

Oh, Susanna

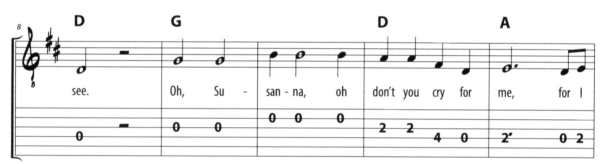

2. *I had a dream the other night*
   when ev'rything was still;
   I thought I saw Susanna
   a-comin' down the hill;
   the buckwheat cake was in her mouth,
   the tear was in her eye;
   says I, I'm comin' from the south,
   Susanna, don't you cry.
   O, Susanna,
   o, don't you cry for me ...

3. *I soon will be in New Orleans,*
   and then I'll look around,
   and when I find Susanna
   I'll fall upon the ground.
   And if I do not find her,
   then I will surely die,
   and when I'm dead and buried,
   Susanna, don't you cry.
   O, Susanna,
   o, don't you cry for me ...

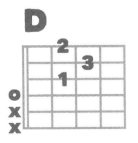

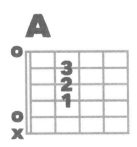

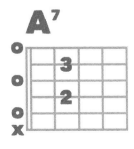

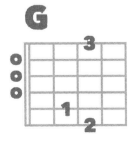

hen the saints go marchin' in

2. And when the stars begin to shine ...

3. And when the band begins to play ...

4. When Gabriel blows in his horn ...

5. And when the sun refuses to shine ...

6. And when they crown Him Lord of Lords ...

7. And on that halleluja-day ...

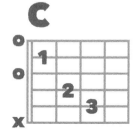
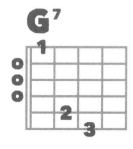
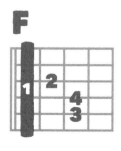
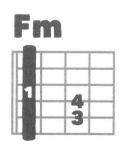

We wish you a merry Christmas

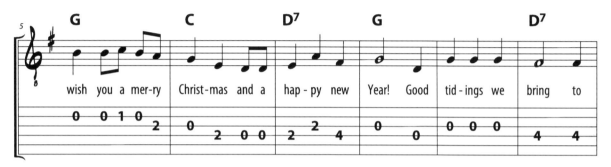

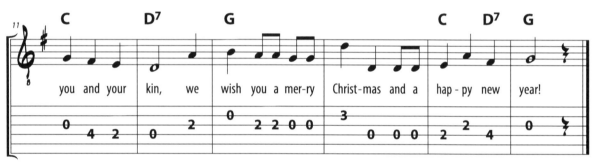

2. Now bring us some figgy pudding (3x)
   And bring some out here!

3. For we all like figgy pudding,
   We all like figgy pudding (2x)
   So bring some out here!

4. And we won't go until we've got some,
   We won't go until we've got some (2x)
   So bring some out here!

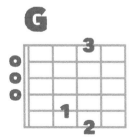
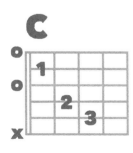
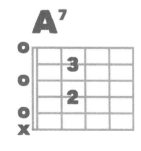
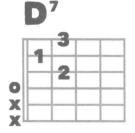

My Bonnie lies over the ocean

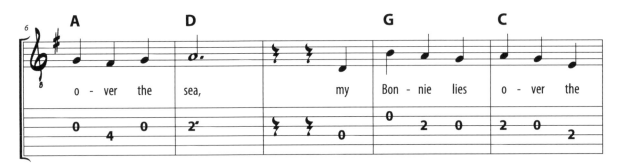

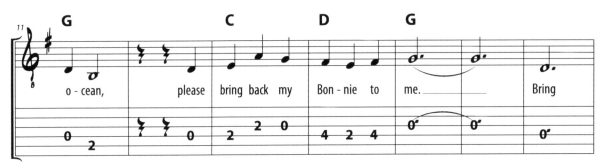

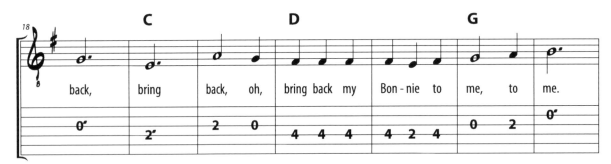

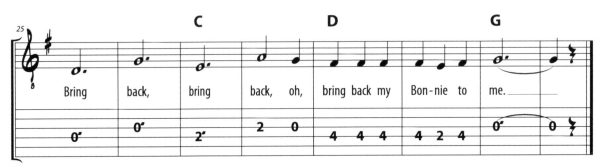

2. *Last night as I lay on my pillow,*
   last night as I lay on my bed.
   Last night as I lay on my pillow,
   I dreamed that my Bonnie was dead,
   Bring back, bring back,
   bring back my Bonnie to me, to me.
   Bring back, bring back,
   bring back my Bonnie to me.

3. *Oh blow ye the winds o'er the ocean,*
   and blow ye the winds o'er the sea.
   Oh blow ye the winds o'er the ocean,
   and bring back my Bonnie to me.
   Bring back, bring back,
   bring back my Bonnie to me, to me.
   Bring back, bring back,
   bring back my Bonnie to me.

4. *The winds have blown over the ocean,*
   the winds have blown over the sea.
   The winds have blown over the ocean,
   and brought back my Bonnie to me.
   Bring back, bring back,
   bring back my Bonnie to me, to me.
   Bring back, bring back,
   bring back my Bonnie to me.

G

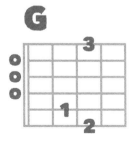

C

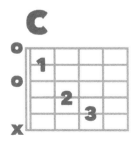

A

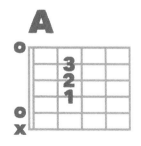

D

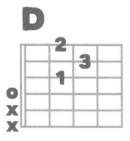

Good night, Ladies

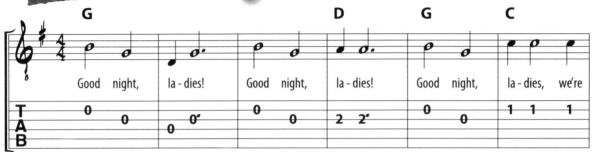

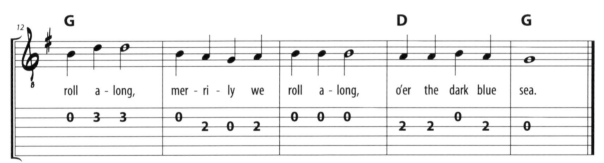

2. Farewell, ladies! (3x)
   We're going to leave you now.
   Merrily we roll along,
   roll along, roll along,
   merrily we roll along,
   o'er the deep blue sea.

3. Sweet dreams, ladies! (3x)
   We're going to leave you now.
   Merrily we roll along,
   roll along, roll along,
   merrily we roll along,
   o'er the deep blue sea.

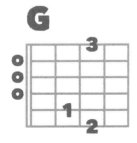
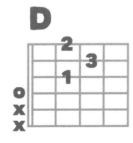
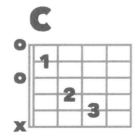

Tom Dooley

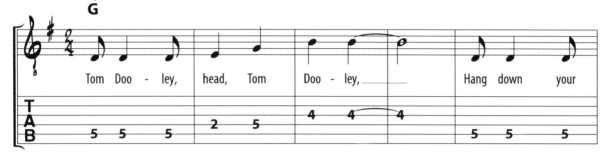

Tom Doo - ley,   head, Tom   Doo - ley, _____   Hang down   your

head   and   cry, _____   Hang   down   your   head,   Tom

Doo - ley, _____   Poor   boy,   you're   bound   to   die.

2. This time tomorrow,
    Reckon where I'll be?
    If it hadn't been for Grayson,
    I'd a-been in Tennesse.

3. This time tomorrow,
    Reckon where I'll be?
    Down in some lonesome valley,
    Hangin' from a white oak tree.

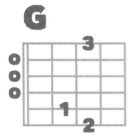

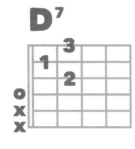

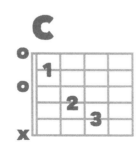

ow, row, row

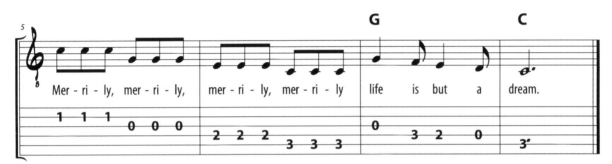

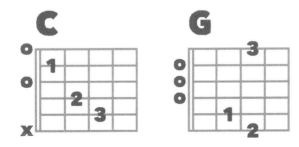

Kum ba yah

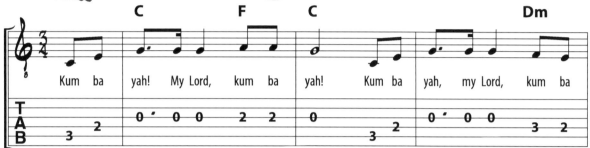

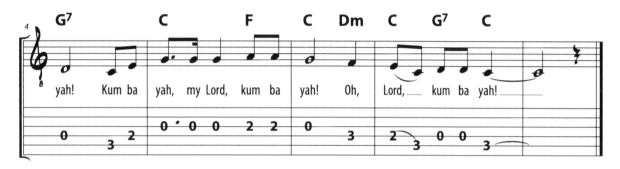

2. Someone's crying, Lord, kum ba yah!

3. Someone's singing, Lord, kum ba yah!

4. Someone's praying, Lord, kum ba yah!

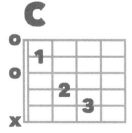
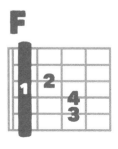
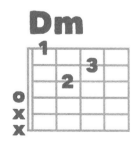
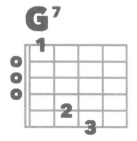

Humpty Dumpty

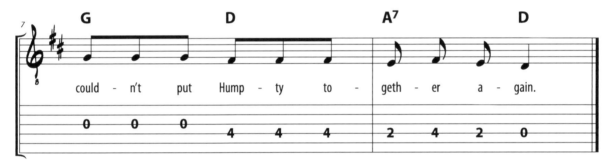

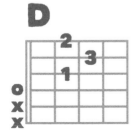

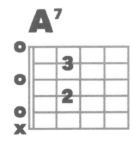

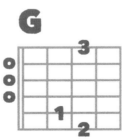

Jack Sprat

	C	G7	C		Am	D7	G
	Jack	Sprat could	eat no fat,	his	wife	could eat no	lean. And

	F		E7	Am	C	G7	C
	so	be-tween them	both, you	see, they	licked	the plat - ter	clean.

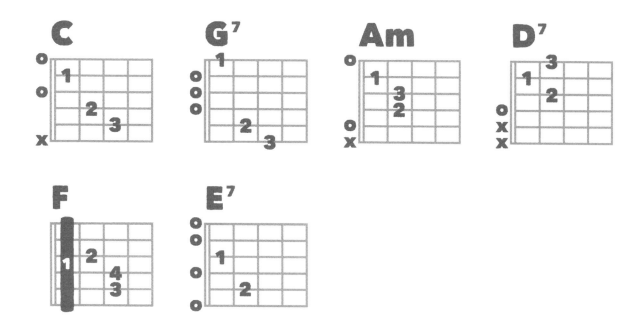

Mary had a little lamb

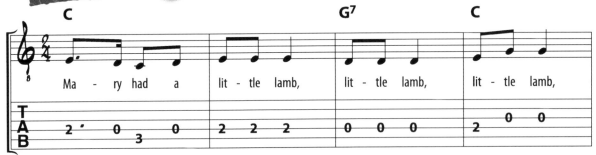

2. And everywhere that Mary went,
   Mary went, Mary went,
   everywhere that Mary went
   the lamb was sure to go.

3. It followed her to school one day,
   school one day, school one day,
   it followed her to school one day
   which was against the rule.

4. It made the children laugh and play,
   laugh and play, laugh and play,
   it made the children laugh and play
   to see a lamb at school.

5. And so the teacher turned it out,
   turned it out, turned it out,
   and so the teacher turned it out
   but still it lingered near.

6. And waited patiently about,
   Patiently, patiently,
   and waited patiently about
   till Mary did appear.

7. "Why does the lamb love Mary so,
   Mary so, Mary so?"
   "Why does the lamb love Mary so?"
   the eager children cry.

8. "Because the lamb loves Mary so,
   Mary so, Mary so",
   "Because the lamb loves Mary so",
   the teacher did reply.

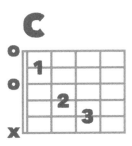

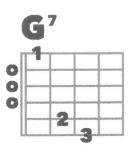

Six little ducks

Six li-ttle ducks that | I once knew, | fat ones, skin-ny ones, | fair ones, too. But the

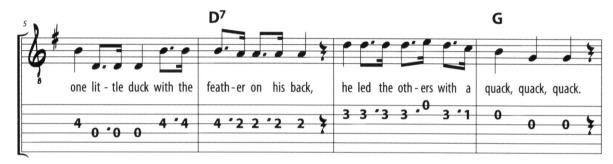

one lit-tle duck with the | feath-er on his back, | he led the oth-ers with a | quack, quack, quack.

Quack, quack, quack, | quack, quack, quack, | he led the oth-ers with a | quack, quack, quack.

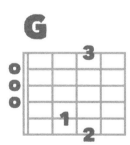

G

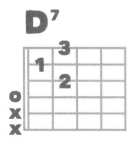

D7

2. *Down to the river they would go,*
   Wibble, wobble, wibble, wobble, to and fro.
   But the one little duck with the feather on his back,
   he led the others with a quack, quack, quack.
   Quack, quack, quack, quack, quack, quack,
   he led the others with a quack, quack, quack.

3. *Back from the river they would come,*
   Wibble, wobble, wibble, wobble, ho, hum, hum.
   But the one little duck with the feather on his back,
   he led the others with a quack, quack, quack.
   Quack, quack, quack, quack, quack, quack,
   he led the others with a quack, quack, quack.

Georgie Porgie

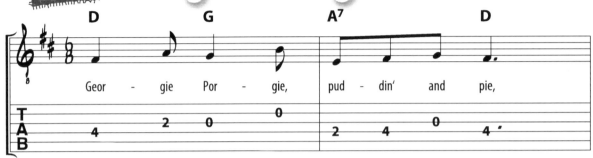

Geor – gie Por – gie, pud – din' and pie,

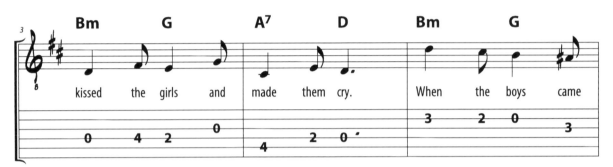

kissed the girls and made them cry. When the boys came

out to play, Geor – gie Por – gie ran a – way.

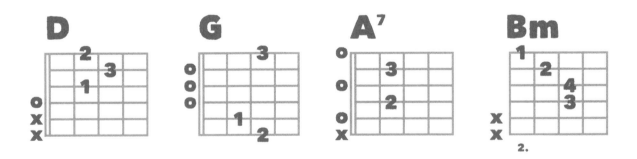

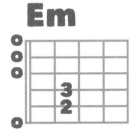

Jack be nimble

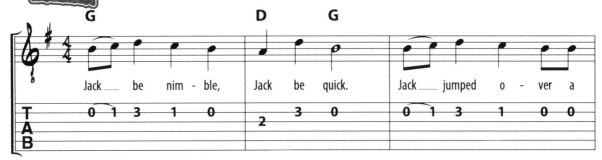

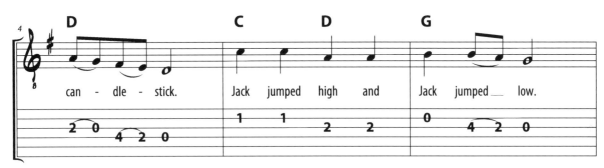

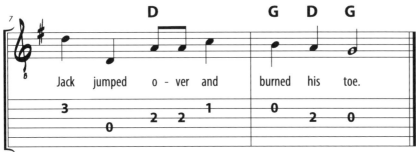

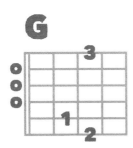

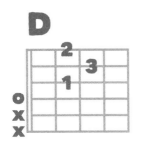

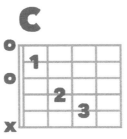

ulberry bush

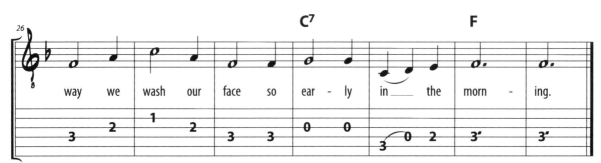

2. *This is the way we comb our hair,*
   we comb our hair, we comb our hair.
   This is the way we comb our hair
   so early in the morning.

4. *This is the way we put on our clothes,*
   we put on our clothes, we put on our clothes.
   This is the way we put on our clothes
   so early in the morning.

3. *This is the way we brush our teeth,*
   we brush our teeth, we brush our teeth.
   This is the way we brush our teeth
   so early in the morning.

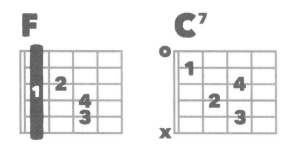

The farmer in the dell

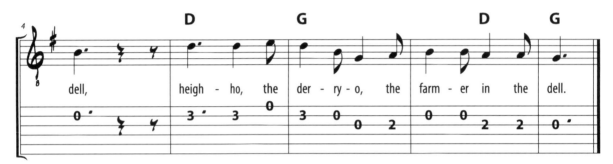

2. The farmer takes the wife (2×)
   Heigh-ho, the derry-o …
   The farmer takes the wife

3. The wife takes the child (2×)
   Heigh-ho, the derry-o …
   The wife takes the child

4. The child takes the nurse (2×)
   Heigh-ho, the derry-o …
   The child takes the nurse

5. The nurse takes the cow (2×)
   Heigh-ho, the derry-o …
   The nurse takes the cow

6. The cow takes the dog (2×)
   Heigh-ho, the derry-o …
   The cow takes the dog

7. The dog takes the cat (2×)
   Heigh-ho, the derry-o …
   The dog takes the cat

8. The cat takes the mouse (2×)
   Heigh-ho, the derry-o …
   The cat takes the mouse

9. The mouse takes the cheese (2×)
   Heigh-ho, the derry-o …
   The mouse takes the cheese

10. The cheese stands alone (2×)
    Heigh-ho, the derry-o …
    The cheese stands alone

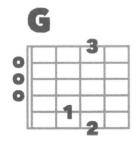

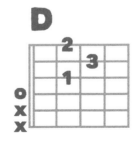

Bye, baby bunting

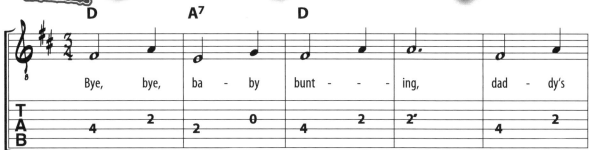

Bye, bye, ba — by bunt — — ing, dad — dy's

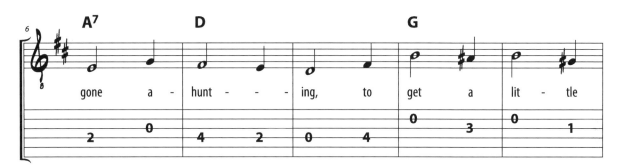

gone a — hunt — — ing, to get a lit — tle

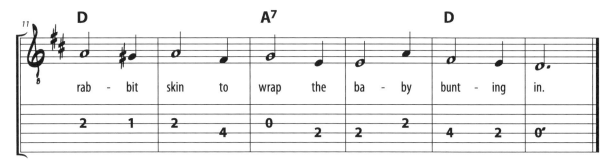

rab — bit skin to wrap the ba — by bunt — ing in.

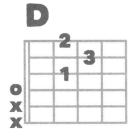

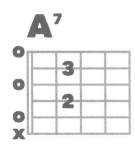

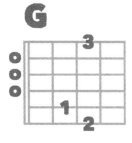

Lucy Locket

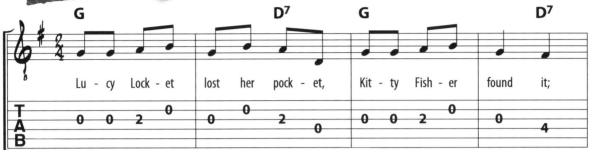

Lu - cy Lock - et | lost her pock - et, | Kit - ty Fish - er | found it;

not a pen - ny | was there in it, | on - ly rib - bon | 'round it.

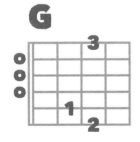
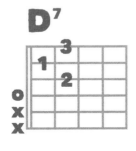
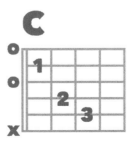

Pease porridge hot

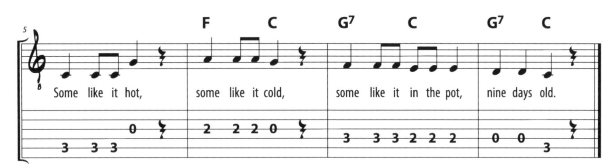

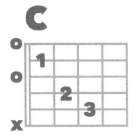

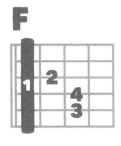

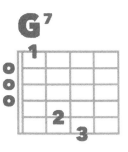

Nobody likes me

No - bod-y likes me,   ev - 'ry-bod - y hates me,   guess I'll go eat   worms.

Long, thin, slim-y ones,   short, fat, juic-y ones,   it-sy, bit-sy, fuz-zy, wuz-zy   worms.

2. Down goes the first one,
   down goes the second one,
   oh, how they wiggle and squirm.
   Long, thin, slimy ones,
   short, fat, juicy ones
   itsy, bitsy, fuzzy, wuzzy worms.

3. Up comes the first one,
   up comes the second one,
   oh, how they wiggle and squirm.
   Long, thin, slimy ones,
   short, fat, juicy ones,
   itsy, bitsy, fuzzy, wuzzy worms.

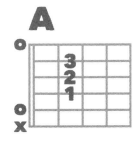

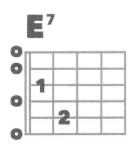

Little Miss Muffet

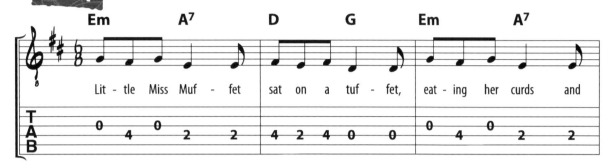

Lit - tle Miss Muf - fet   sat on a tuf - fet,   eat - ing her curds and

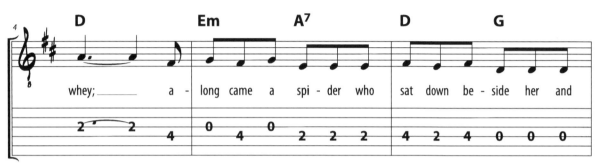

whey; _____   a - long came a spi - der who   sat down be - side her and

fright - ened Miss Muff - et a - way. _____

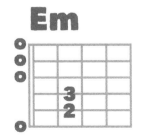
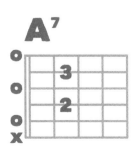
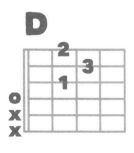
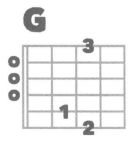

Pat-a-cake

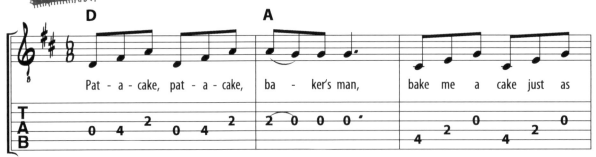

Pat - a - cake, pat - a - cake, ba - ker's man, bake me a cake just as

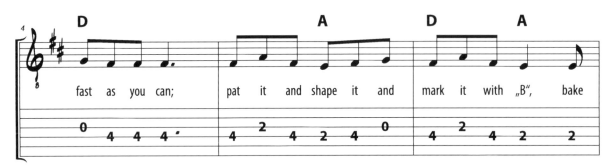

fast as you can; pat it and shape it and mark it with „B", bake

it in the o - ven for ba - by and me, for ba - by and me, for

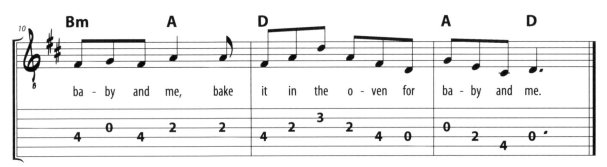

ba - by and me, bake it in the o - ven for ba - by and me.

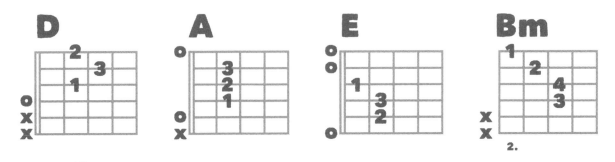

Peter, Peter, pumpkin eater

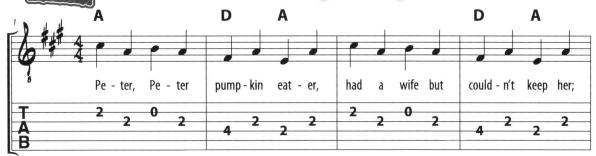

Pe - ter, Pe - ter pump - kin eat - er, had a wife but could - n't keep her;

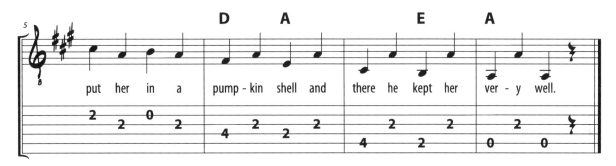

put her in a pump - kin shell and there he kept her ver - y well.

2. Peter, Peter, pumpkin eater,
   had another and didn't love her;
   Peter learned to read and spell,
   and then he loved her very well.

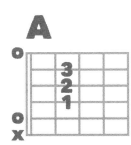

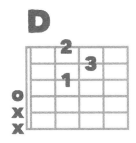

There was a crooked man

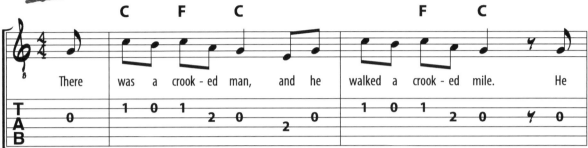

There was a crook-ed man, and he walked a crook-ed mile. He

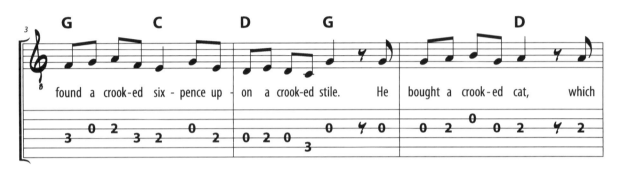

found a crook-ed six-pence up-on a crook-ed stile. He bought a crook-ed cat, which

caught a crook-ed mouse, and they all lived to-geth-er in a lit-tle crook-ed house.

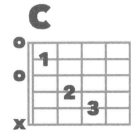

C

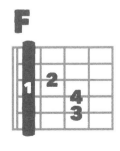

F

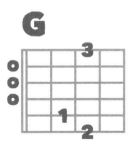

G

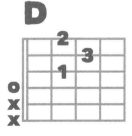

D

Lazy Mary

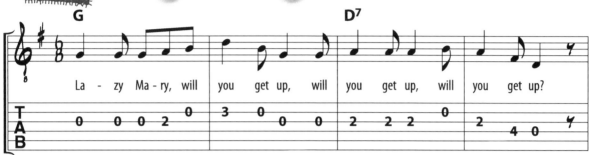

La - zy Ma - ry, will you get up, will you get up, will you get up?

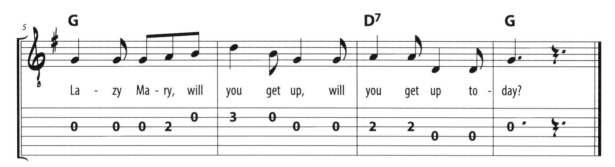

La - zy Ma - ry, will you get up, will you get up to - day?

2. *No, no, mother I won't get up,*
   I won't get up, I won't get up.
   No, no, mother I won't get up,
   I won't get up today.

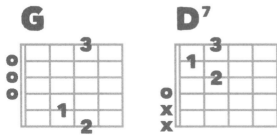

Over in the meadow

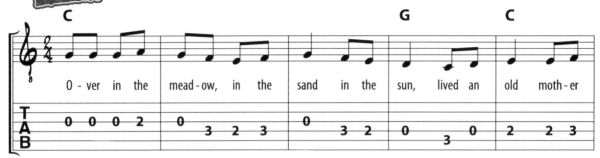

Over in the mead-ow, in the sand in the sun, lived an old moth-er

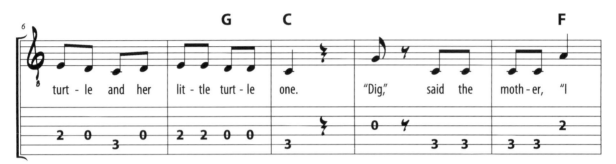

turt-le and her lit-tle turt-le one. "Dig," said the moth-er, "I

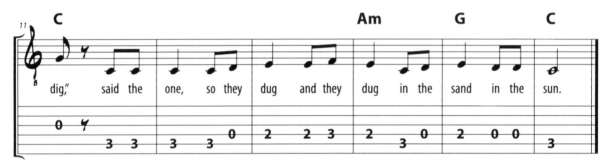

dig," said the one, so they dug and they dug in the sand in the sun.

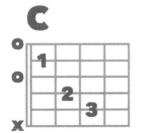

C

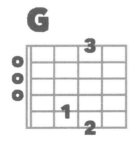

G

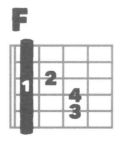

F

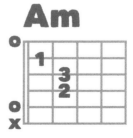

Am

2.   Over in the meadow where the stream runs blue,
     lived an old mother fish and her little fishies two.
     "Swim," said the mother, "We swim," said the two,
     so they swam and they swam where the stream runs blue.

3.   Over in the meadow in a hole in the tree,
     Lived an old mother owl and her little owls three.
     "Whoo," said the mother, "We whoo," said the three,
     so they whooed and they whooed in the hole in the tree.

4.   Over in the meadow by the old barn door,
     Lived an old mother rat and her little ratties four.
     "Gnaw," said the mother, "We gnaw," said the four,
     so they gnawed and the gnawed by the old barn door.

5.   Over in the meadow in a snug beehive,
     Lived an old mother bee and her little bees five.
     "Buzz," said the mother, "We buzz," said the five,
     so they buzzed and they buzzed in the snug beehive.

6.   Over in the meadow in a nest built of sticks,
     Lived an old mother crow and her little crows six.
     "Caw," said the mother, "We caw," said the six,
     so they cawed and the cawed in the nest built of sticks.

7.   Over in the meadow where the grass grows so even,
     Lived an old mother frog and her little froggies seven.
     "Jump," said the mother, "We jump," said the seven,
     so they jumped and they jumped where the grass grows so even.

8.   Over in the meadow by the old mossy gate,
     Lived an old mother lizard and her little lizards eight.
     "Bask," said the mother, "We bask," said the eight,
     so they basked and they basked by the old mossy gate.

9.   Over in the meadow by the old scotch pine,
     Lived an old mother duck and her little duckies nine.
     "Quack," said the mother, "We quack," said the nine,
     so they quacked and they quacked by the old scotch pine.

10. Over in the meadow in a cozy, wee den,
     Lived an old mother beaver and her little beavers ten.
     "Beave," said the mother, "We beave," said the ten,
     so they beaved and they beaved in their cozy, wee den.

Three little kittens

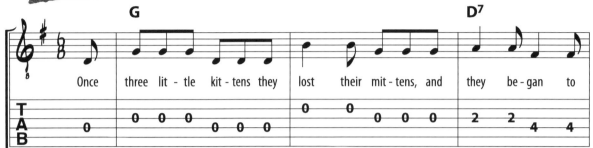

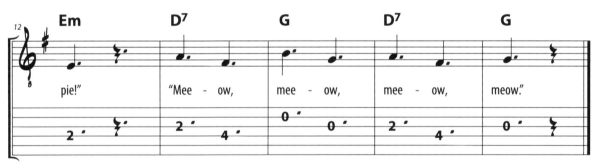

2. *The three little kittens they found their mittens,*
   and they began to cry,
   "Oh, mother dear, see here, see here,
   we have found our mittens."
   "Put on your mittens, you silly kittens,
   and you shall have some pie."
   "Mee-ow, mee-ow, mee-ow."

3. *The three little kittens put on their mittens,*
   and soon ate up the pie;
   "Oh, mother dear, we greatly fear
   we have soiled our mittens."
   "What! soiled your mittens, you naughty kittens!"
   Then they began to sigh,
   "Mee-ow, mee-ow, mee-ow."

4. *The three little kittens they washed their mittens,*
   and hung them out to dry;
   "Oh! mother dear, do you not hear,
   we have washed our mittens."
   "What! washed your mittens, then you're good kittens,
   But I smell a rat close by."
   "Mee-ow, mee-ow, mee-ow."

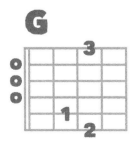
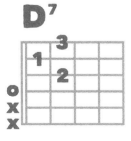
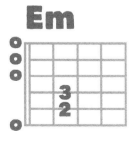
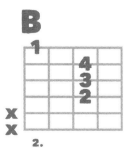

Animal fair

C   **G7**

I went to the an-i-mal fair,   the birds and beasts were there,

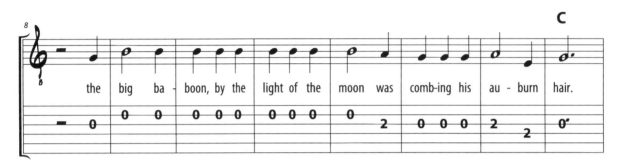

C

the big ba-boon, by the light of the moon was comb-ing his au-burn hair.

G7

The mon-key bumped the skunk,   and sat on the el-e-phant's trunk.

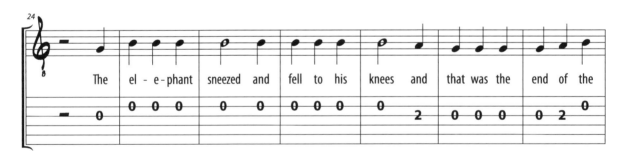

The el-e-phant sneezed and fell to his knees and that was the end of the

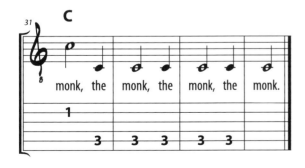

C

monk, the monk, the monk, the monk.

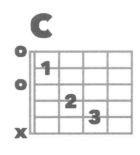

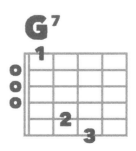

See-saw, Margery Daw

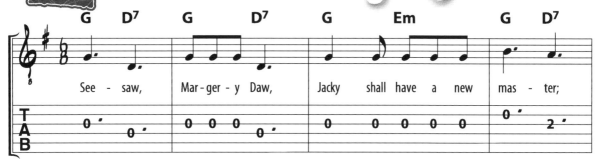

See - saw, Mar-ger-y Daw, Jacky shall have a new mas - ter;

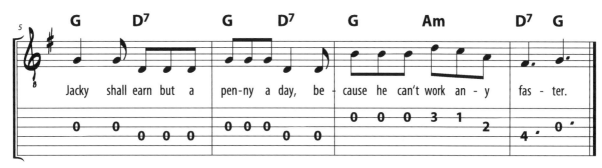

Jacky shall earn but a pen-ny a day, be - cause he can't work an - y fas - ter.

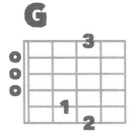

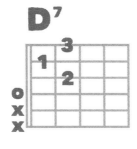

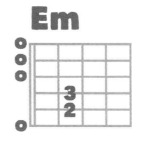

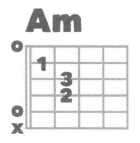

All the pretty little horses

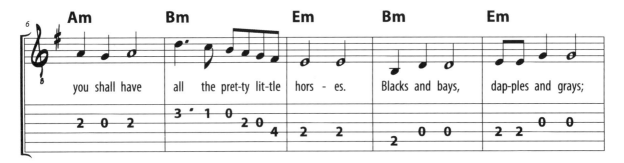

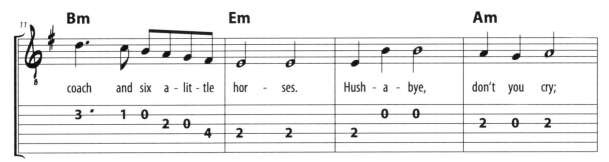

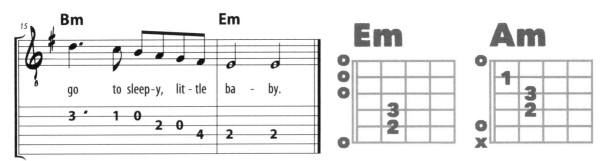

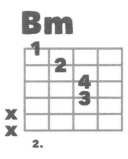

2. Hush-a-bye, don't you cry; go to sleepy, little baby.
   When you wake you shall have all the pretty little horses.
   Paint and Bay, sorrel and gray, all the pretty little ponies.
   Hush-a-bye, don't you cry; go to sleepy, little baby.

3. Hush-a-bye, don't you cry; go to sleepy, little baby.
   When you wake you shall have all the pretty little horses.
   Way down under the meadow lies a poor little lambie.
   Hush-a-bye, don't you cry; go to sleepy, little baby.

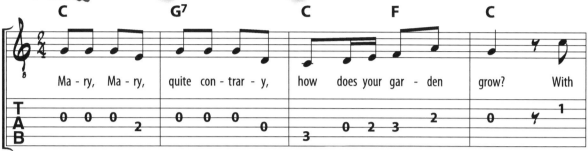

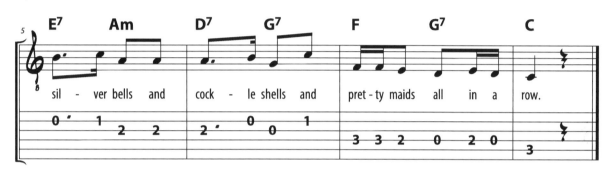

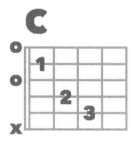

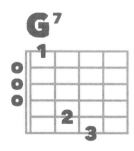

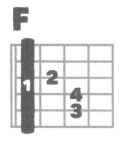

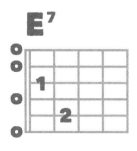

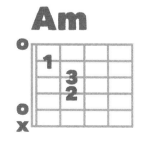

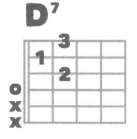

Polly put the kettle on

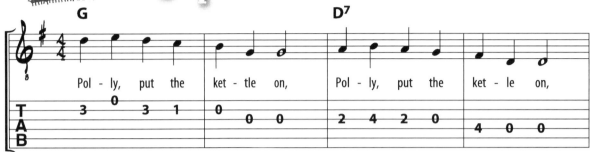

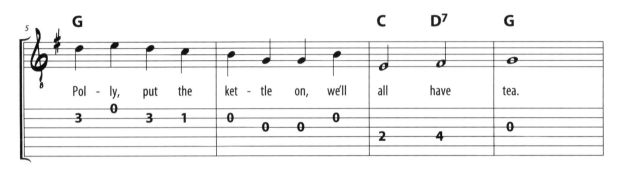

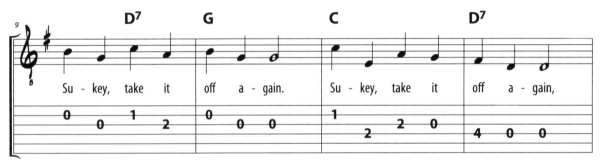

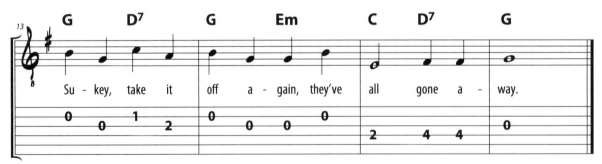

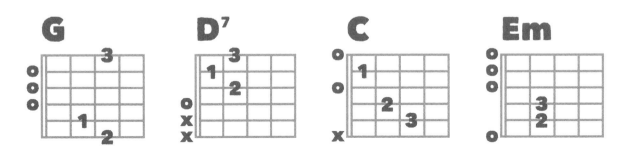

Away in a manger

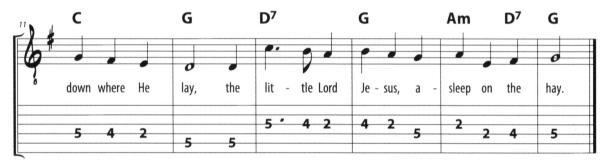

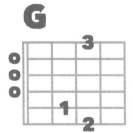

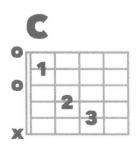

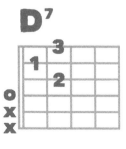

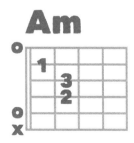

Good King Wenceslas

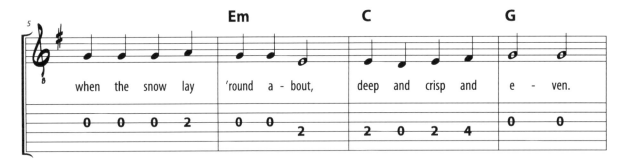

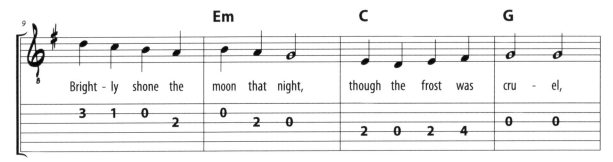

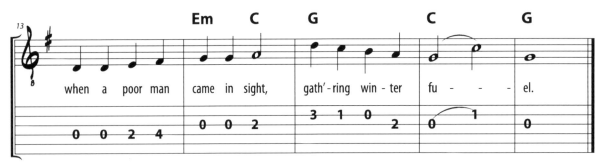

2. "Hither, page, and stand by me, if thou know'st it, telling;
Yonder peasant, who is he? Where and what his dwelling?"
"Sire, he lives a good league hence, underneath the mountain;
Right against the forest fence, by Saint Agnes' fountain."

3. "Bring me flesh, and bring me wine, bring me pine logs hither:
Thou and I shall see him dine, when we bear them thither."
Page and monarch, forth they went, forth they went together;
Through the rude wind's wild lament and the bitter weather.

4. "Sire, the night is darker now, and the wind blows stronger;
Fails my heart, I know not how; I can go no longer."
"Mark my footsteps, good my page. Tread thou in them boldly
Thou shalt find the winter's rage freeze thy blood less coldly."

5. In his master's steps he trod, where the snow lay dinted;
Heat was in the very sod which the saint had printed.
Therefore, Christian men, be sure, wealth or rank possessing,
Ye who now will bless the poor, shall yourselves find blessing.

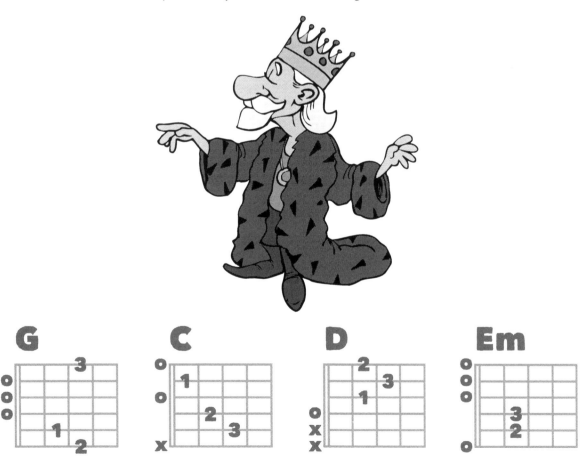

Hark! The herald angels sing

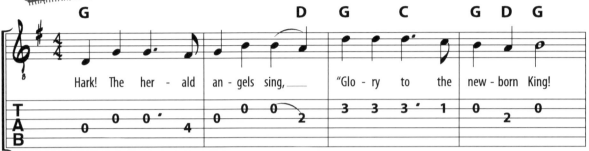

Hark! The her - ald an - gels sing,___ "Glo - ry to the new - born King!

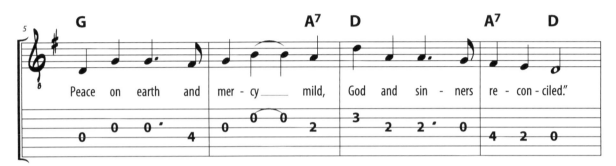

Peace on earth and mer - cy___ mild, God and sin - ners re - con - ciled."

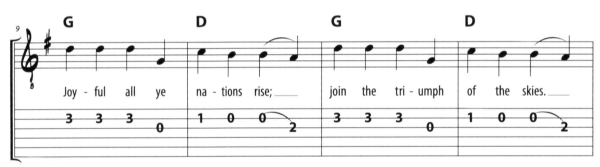

Joy - ful all ye na - tions rise;___ join the tri - umph of the skies.___

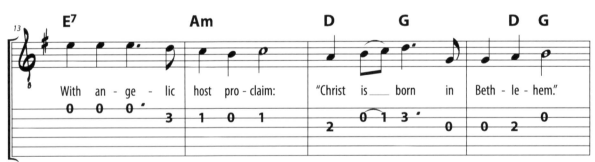

With an - ge - lic host pro - claim: "Christ is___ born in Beth - le - hem."

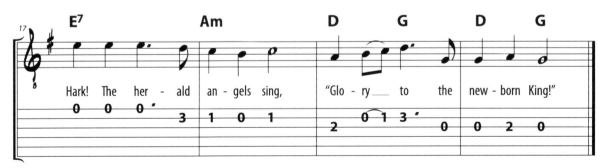

Hark! The her - ald an - gels sing, "Glo - ry___ to the new - born King!"

2. Christ by highest heav'n adored,
   Christ the everlasting Lord!
   Late in time behold Him come,
   Offspring of a Virgin's womb.
   Veiled in flesh the Godhead see
   Hail the incarnate Deity!
   Pleased as man with man to dwell,
   Jesus, our Emmanuel.
   Hark! The herald angels sing
   "Glory to the newborn King!"

3. Hail the heav'n-born Prince of Peace!
   Hail the Son of Righteousness!
   Light and life to all He brings,
   Ris'n with healing in His wings.
   Mild He lays His glory by
   Born that man no more may die.
   Born to raise the sons of earth,
   Born to give them second birth.
   Hark! The herald angels sing
   "Glory to the newborn King!"

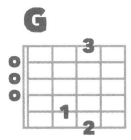
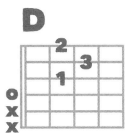
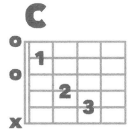
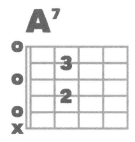

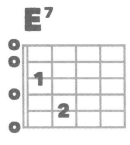
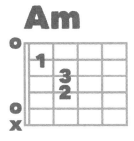

O holy night

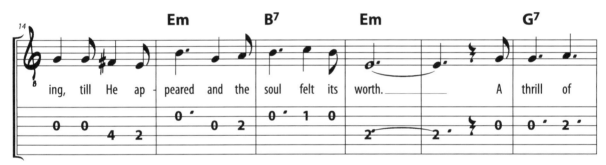

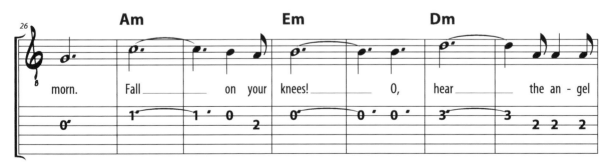

voic - es! O night di - vine, O night

when Christ was born! O night, O Ho - ly night,

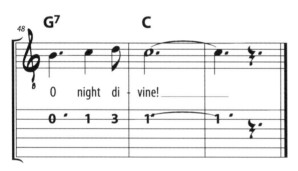

O night di - vine!

2. Led by the light of faith serenely beaming,
   with glowing hearts by His cradle we stand.
   O'er the world a star is sweetly gleaming,
   now come the wisemen from out of the Orient land.
   The King of kings lay thus lowly manger;
   In all our trials born to be our friends.
   He knows our need, our weakness is no stranger,
   behold your King! Before him lowly bend!

3. Truly He taught us to love one another,
   His law is love and His gospel is peace.
   Chains he shall break, for the slave is our brother.
   And in his name all oppression shall cease.
   Sweet hymns of joy in grateful chorus raise we,
   with all our hearts we praise His holy name.
   Christ is the Lord! Then ever, ever praise we,
   His power and glory ever more proclaim!

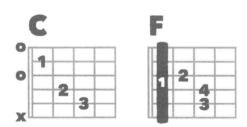

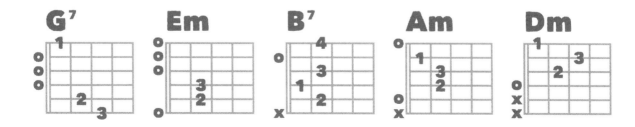

Toyland

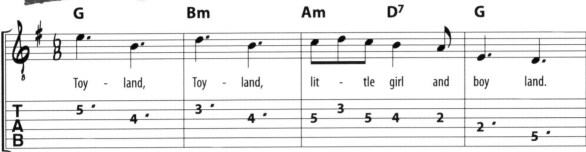

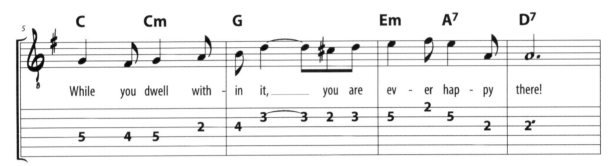

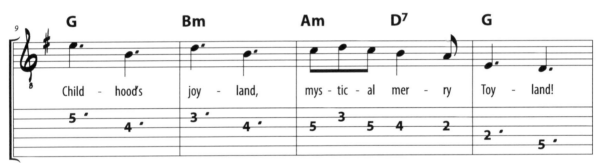

G

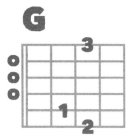

Bm

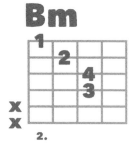

2.

Am

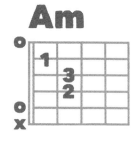

D⁷

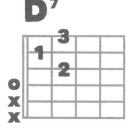

C

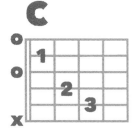

Cm

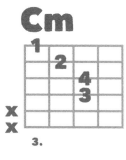

3.

Em

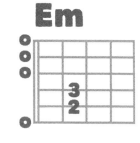

A⁷

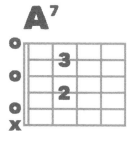

E⁷

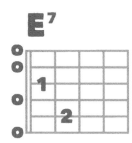

Aura Lee

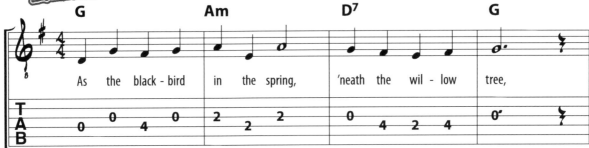

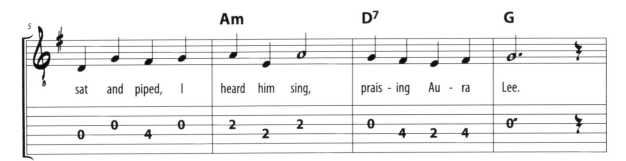

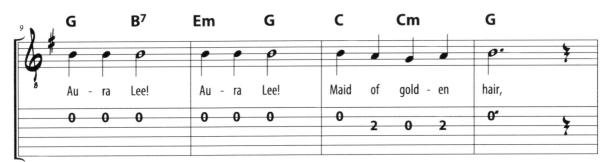

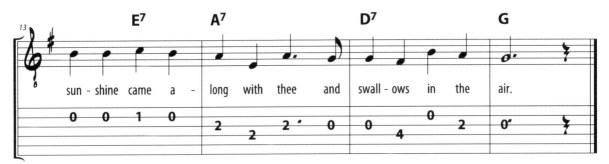

2. *In thy blush the rose was born,*
   music, when you spake.
   Through thine azure eye the morn,
   sparkling seemed to break.
   Aura Lea, Aura Lea,
   birds of crimson wing,
   never song have sung to me,
   as in that sweet spring.
   Aura Lee! Aura Lee! ...

3. *Aura Lea! The bird may flee,*
   the willow's golden hair
   swing through winter fitfully,
   on the stormy air.
   Yet if thy blue eyes I see,
   gloom will soon depart;
   For to me, sweet Aura Lea
   is sunshine through the heart.
   Aura Lee! Aura Lee! ...

4. When the mistletoe was green,
   Midst the winter's snows,
   Sunshine in thy face was seen,
   Kissing lips of rose.
   Aura Lea, Aura Lea,
   Take my golden ring;
   Love and light return with thee,
   And swallows with the spring.
   Aura Lee! Aura Lee! ...

G

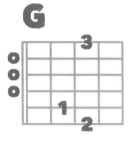

Am

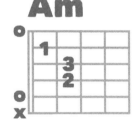

D⁷

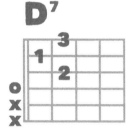

B⁷

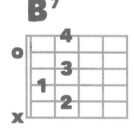

Em

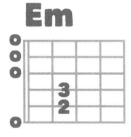

C

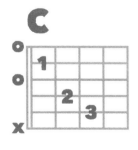

Cm

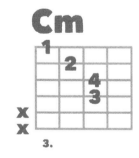

3.

E⁷

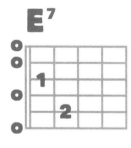

A⁷

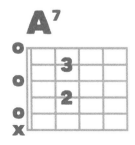

Down by the station

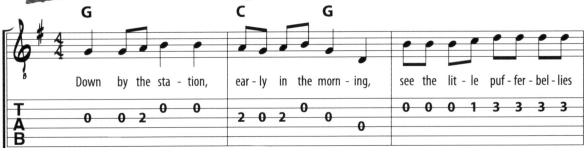

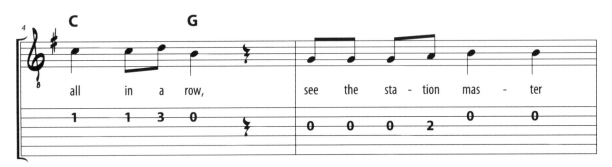

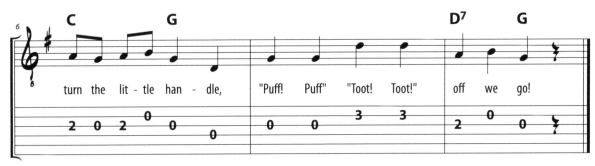

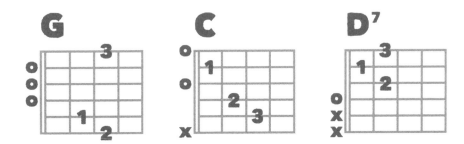

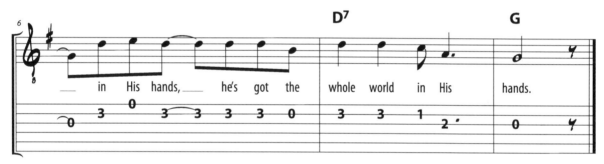

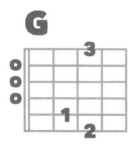

2. He's got the tiny little baby in his hands.

3. He's got you and me brother in his hands.

4. He's got the son and the father in his hands.

5. He's got the mother and her daughter in his hands.

6. He's got everybody here in his hands.

7. He's got the sun and the moon in his hands.

8. He's got the whole world in his hands.

Joshua fit the battle of Jericho

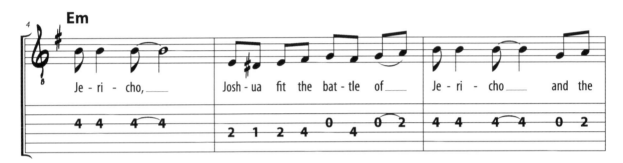

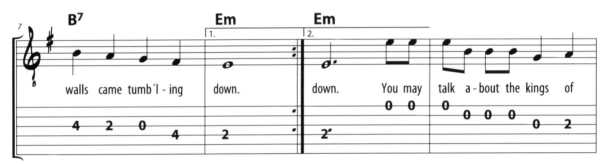

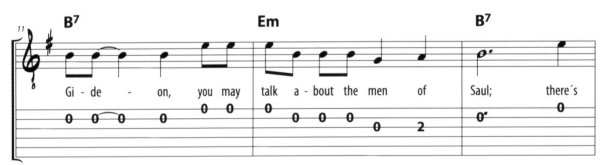

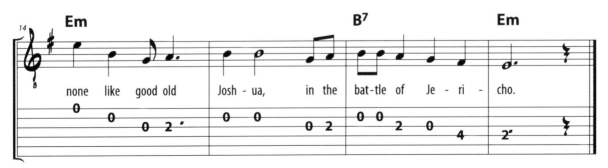

2. Right up to the walls of Jericho,
   he marched with spear in Hand.
   Go, blow dat ram's horn, Joshua cried,
   'cause de battle am in my hand.

3. Then de lamb ram sheep horns begin a blow.
   Trumpets begin to sound.
   Joshua commanded de children to shout,
   and de walls came tumbling down.

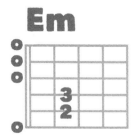

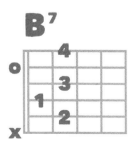

Little brown jug

C · F · G7

My wife and I live all a - lone, in a lit - tle hut we

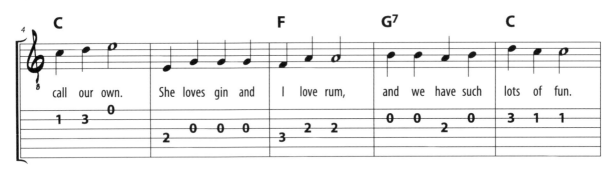

C · F · G7 · C

call our own. She loves gin and I love rum, and we have such lots of fun.

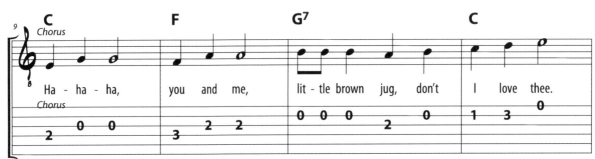

C · F · G7 · C

Chorus

Ha - ha - ha, you and me, lit - tle brown jug, don't I love thee.

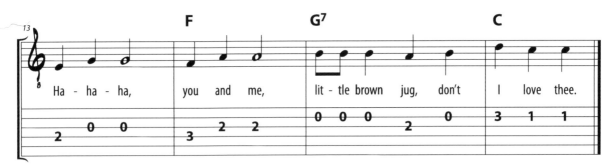

F · G7 · C

Ha - ha - ha, you and me, lit - tle brown jug, don't I love thee.

2. When I go toiling on the farm
   I take the little jug under my arm;
   Place it under a shady tree,
   Little brown jug, 'tis you and me.

3. 'Tis you that makes me friends and foes,
   'Tis you that makes me wear old clothes;
   But, seeing you're so near my nose,
   Tip her up and down she goes.

4. If all the folks in Adam's race
   Were gathered together in one place,
   I'd let them go without a tear
   Before I'd part from you, my dear.

5. If I'd a cow that gave such milk,
   I'd dress her in the finest silk;
   Feed her up on oats and hay,
   And milk her twenty times a day.

6. I bought a cow from Farmer Jones,
   And she was nothing but skin and bones;
   I fed her up as fine as silk,
   She jumped the fence and strained her milk.

7. And when I die don't bury me at all,
   Just pickle my bones in alcohol;
   Put a bottle o' booze at my head and feet
   And then I know that I will keep.

8. The rose is red, my nose is too,
   The violet's blue and so are you;
   And yet, I guess, before I stop,
   We'd better take another drop.

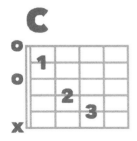

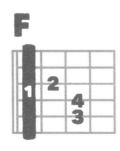

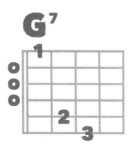

Alouette

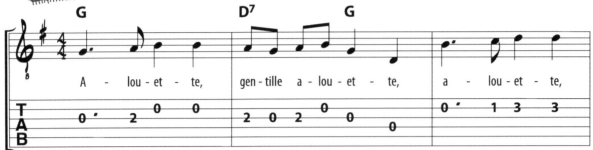

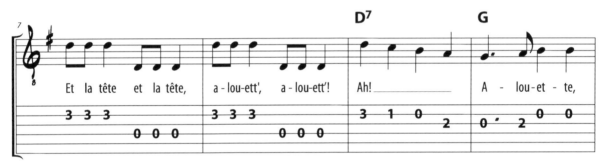

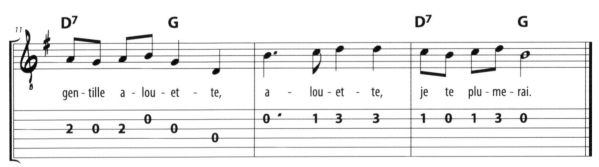

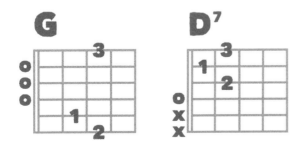

Michael, row the boat ashore

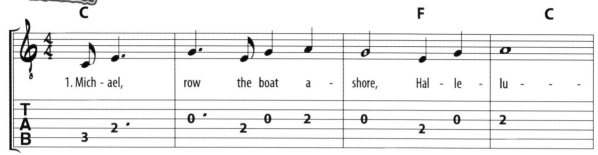

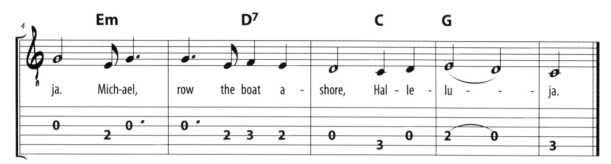

2. Michael boat a gospelboat, Halleluja ...

3. Brother lend a helping hand, Halleluja ...

4. Sister help to trim the sail, Halleluja ...

5. Boasting talk will sink your soul, Halleluja ...

6. Jordan-stream is deep and wide, Halleluja ...

7. Jesus stand on the other side, Halleluja ...

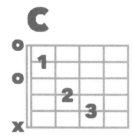
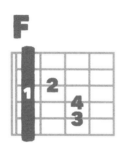
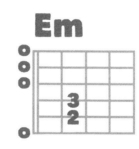
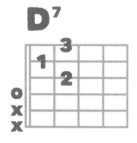

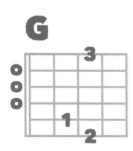

Scarborough Fair

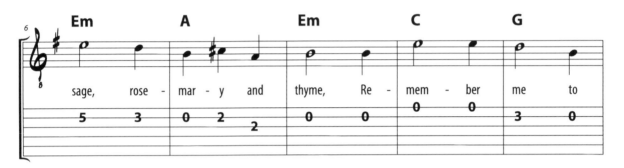

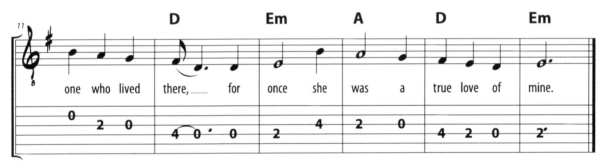

Tell her to make me a cambric shirt,
Parsley, sage, rosemary, and thyme;
Without a seam or needlework,
Then she shall be a true lover of mine.

Tell her to wash it in yonder well,
Parsley, sage, rosemary, and thyme;
Where never spring water or rain ever fell,
And she shall be a true lover of mine.

Tell her to dry it on yonder thorn,
Parsley, sage, rosemary, and thyme;
Which never bore blossom since Adam was born,
Then she shall be a true lover of mine.

Now he has asked me questions three,
Parsley, sage, rosemary, and thyme;
I hope he'll answer as many for me
Before he shall be a true lover of mine.

Tell him to buy me an acre of land,
Parsley, sage, rosemary, and thyme;
Between the salt water and the sea sand,
Then he shall be a true lover of mine.

Tell him to plough it with a ram's horn,
Parsley, sage, rosemary, and thyme;
And sow it all over with one pepper corn,
And he shall be a true lover of mine.

Tell him to sheer't with a sickle of leather,
Parsley, sage, rosemary, and thyme;
And bind it up with a peacock feather.
And he shall be a true lover of mine.

Tell him to thrash it on yonder wall,
Parsley, sage, rosemary, and thyme,
And never let one corn of it fall,
Then he shall be a true lover of mine.

When he has done and finished his work.
Parsley, sage, rosemary, and thyme:
Oh, tell him to come and he'll have his shirt,
And he shall be a true lover of mine.

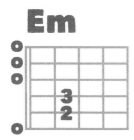

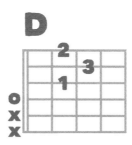

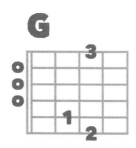

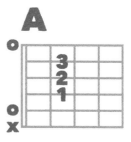

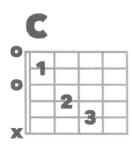

Do your ears hang low?

Do your ears hang low? Do they wob-ble to and fro? Can you

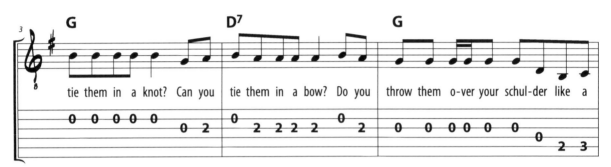

tie them in a knot? Can you tie them in a bow? Do you throw them o-ver your schul-der like a

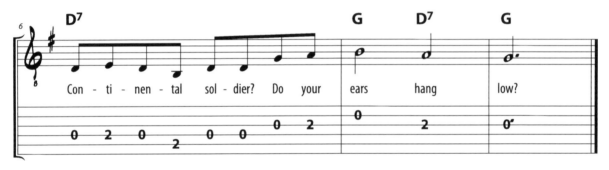

Con - ti - nen - tal sol - dier? Do your ears hang low?

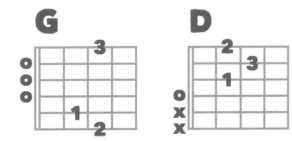

G   **D**

The riddle song

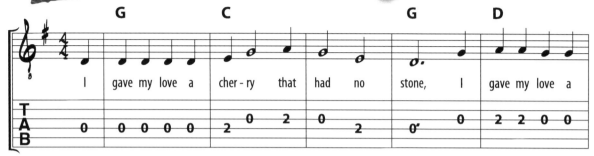

I gave my love a cher-ry that had no stone, I gave my love a

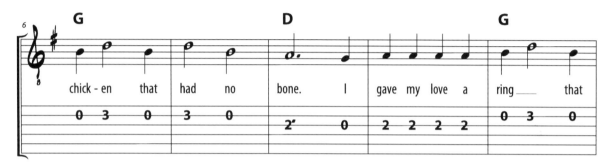

chick-en that had no bone. I gave my love a ring_____ that

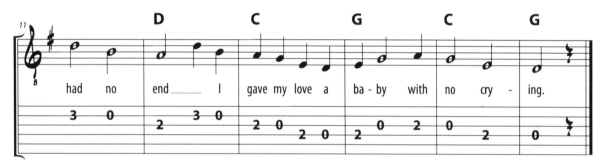

had no end_____ I gave my love a ba-by with no cry - ing.

2. How can there be a cherry
   That has no stone?
   And how can there be a chicken
   That has no bone?
   And how can there be a story
   That has no end?
   And how can there be a baby
   With no crying?

3. A cherry when it's blooming
   It has no stone
   A chicken when it's piping
   It has no bone
   The story that I love you
   It has no end
   A baby when it's sleeping
   It's no crying.

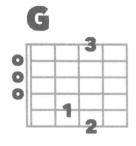

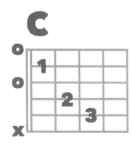

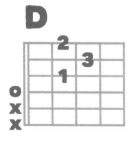

A-Hunting we will go

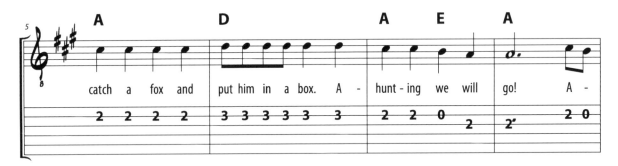

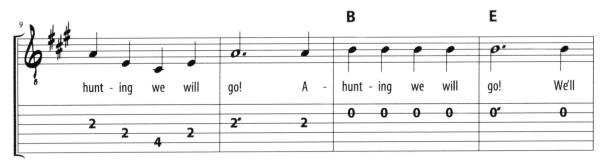

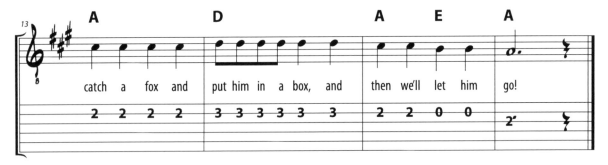

"... a fish and put him on a dish ..."
"... a bear and cut his hair ..."
"... a pig and dance a little jig ..."
"... a giraffe and make him laugh ..."
"... a mouse and put him in a house ..."

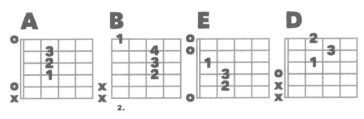

Bill Grogan's goat

Bill Gro-gan's goat was feel-ing fine, ate three red

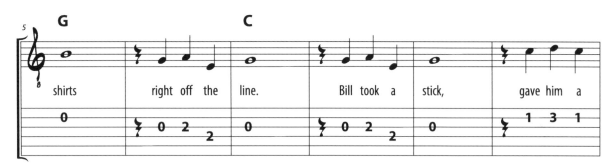

shirts right off the line. Bill took a stick, gave him a

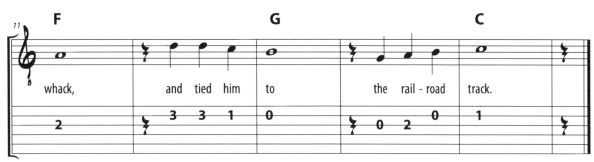

whack, and tied him to the rail-road track.

2. The whistle blew, the train was nigh,
   Bill Grogan's goat was doomed to die!
   He gave a cough of mortal pain,
   coughed up those shirts and flagged the train!

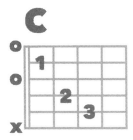

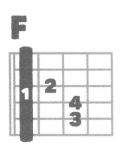

All through the night

Sleep, my child, and peace at-tend thee, all through the night;

Guard – ian an – gels God will send thee, all through the night.

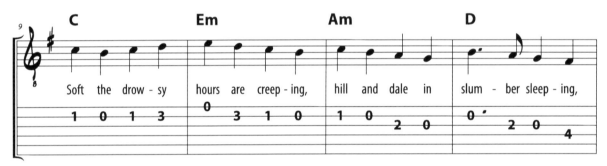

Soft the drow – sy hours are creep – ing, hill and dale in slum – ber sleep – ing,

I my loved ones' watch am keep – ing, all through the night.

2. *While the moon her watch is keeping,*
   all through the night;
   While the weary world is sleeping,
   all through the night.
   O'er thy spirit gently stealing,
   visions of delight revealing,
   breathes a pure and holy feeling,
   all through the night.

G

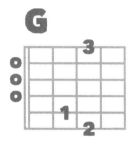

C

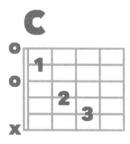

A⁷

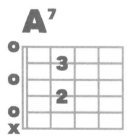

D

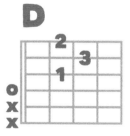

Em

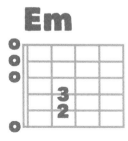

Am

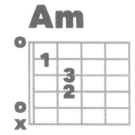

Old King Cole

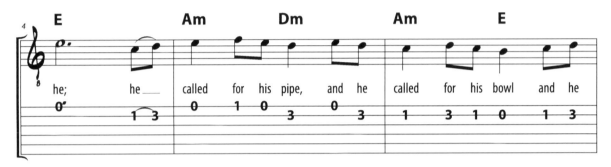

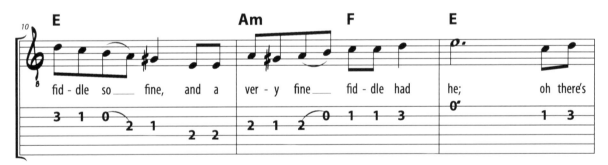

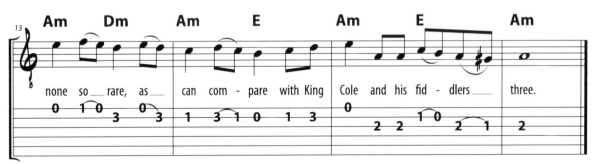

Am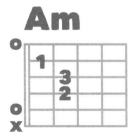

E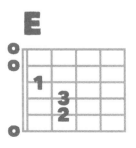

F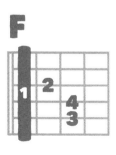

Dm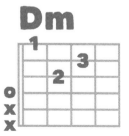

It's raining, it's pouring

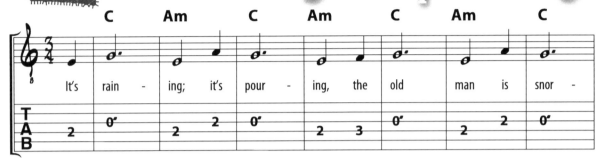

It's rain - ing; it's pour - ing, the old man is snor -

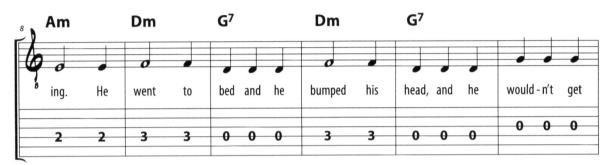

ing. He went to bed and he bumped his head, and he would - n't get

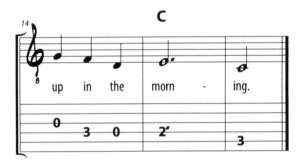

up in the morn - ing.

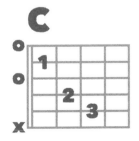

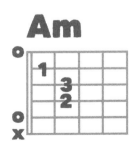

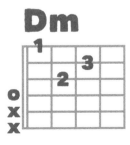

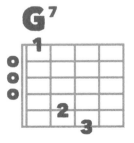

Oh were, oh where has my little dog gone?

Oh where, oh where has my lit-tle dog gone? Oh

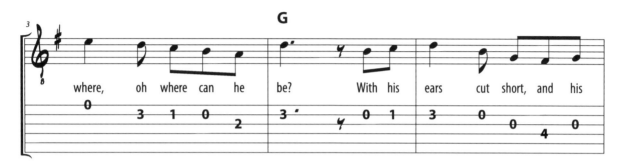

where, oh where can he be? With his ears cut short, and his

tail cut long, Oh where, oh where can he be?

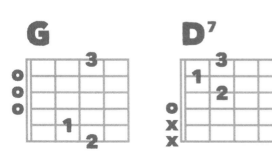

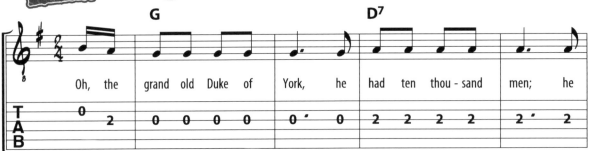

Oh, the grand old Duke of York, he had ten thou - sand men; he

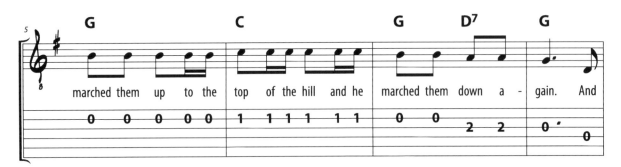

marched them up to the top of the hill and he marched them down a - gain. And

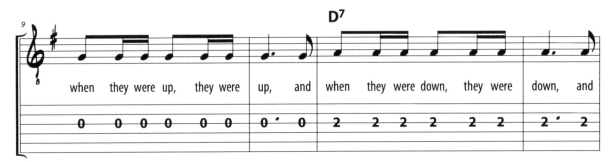

when they were up, they were up, and when they were down, they were down, and

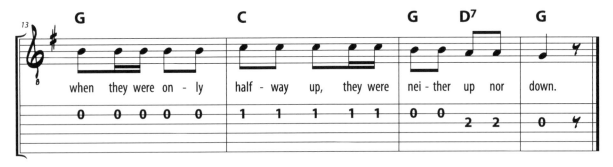

when they were on - ly half - way up, they were nei - ther up nor down.

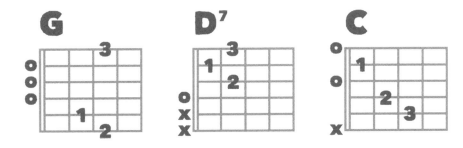

his little pig went to market

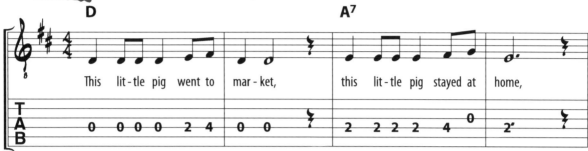

This lit-tle pig went to mar-ket, this lit-tle pig stayed at home,

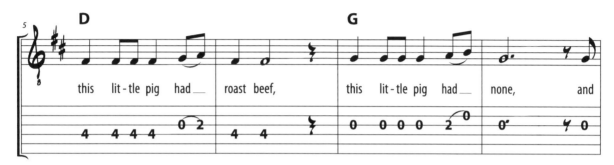

this lit-tle pig had — roast beef, this lit-tle pig had — none, and

this lit-tle pig went wee wee wee wee wee all the way home.

D

A⁷   **G**

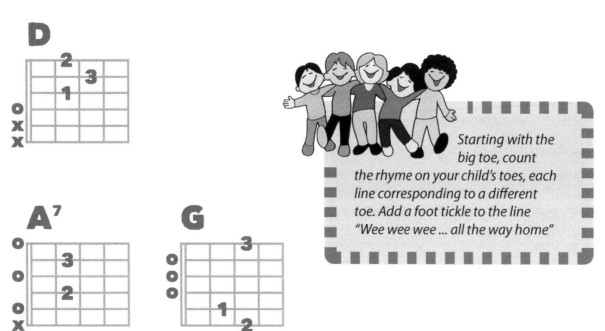

Starting with the big toe, count the rhyme on your child's toes, each line corresponding to a different toe. Add a foot tickle to the line "Wee wee wee ... all the way home"

One, two, buckle my shoe

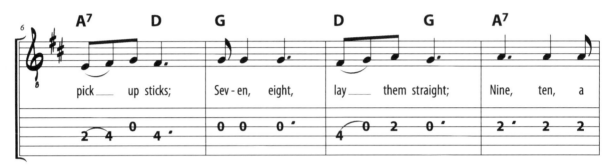

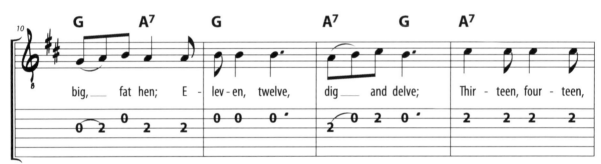

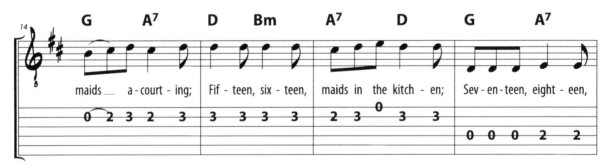

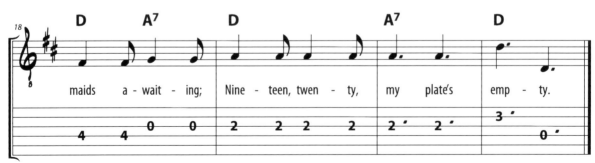

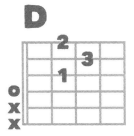

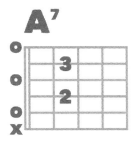

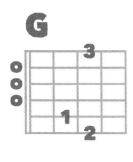

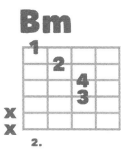

Hot cross buns

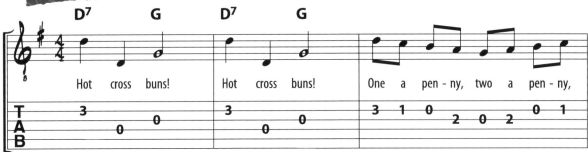

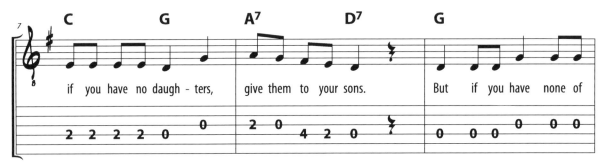

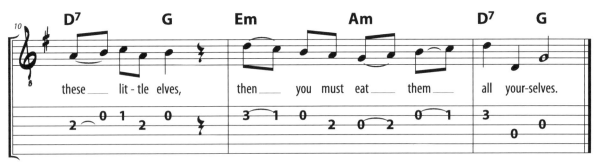

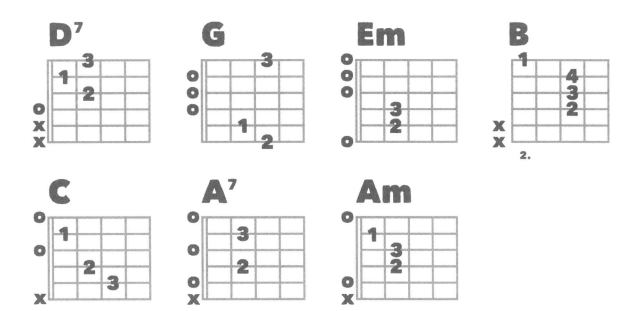

The Hokey Pokey

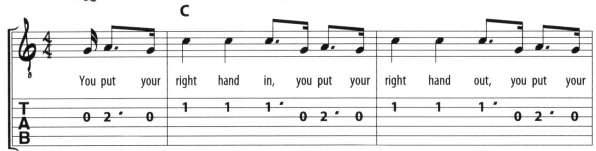

You put your right hand in, you put your right hand out, you put your

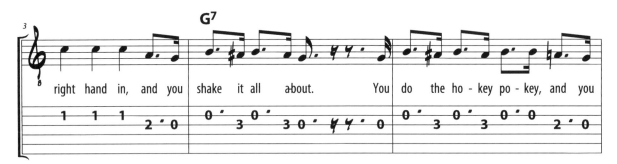

right hand in, and you shake it all about. You do the ho - key po - key, and you

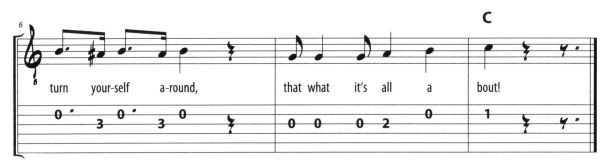

turn your-self a-round, that what it's all a bout!

You put your left hand in ...
You put your right foot in ...
You put your left foot in ...
You put your right shoulder in ...
You put your left shoulder in ...

You put your right hip in ...
You put your left hip in ...
You put your head in ...
You put your whole self in ...

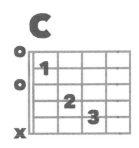

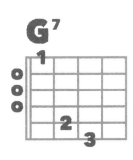

All children stand in a circle and imitate the actions of the words.

Five little ducks

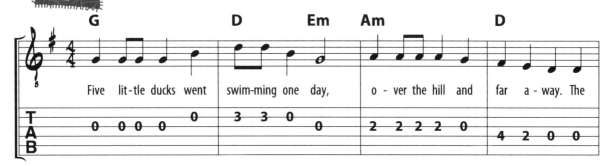

Five lit-tle ducks went | swim-ming one day, | o - ver the hill and | far a - way. The

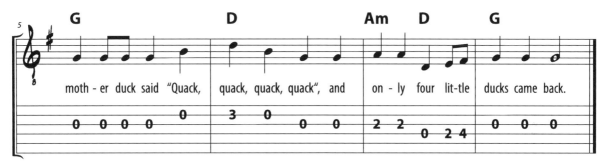

moth - er duck said "Quack, | quack, quack, quack", and | on - ly four lit-tle | ducks came back.

2. Four little ducks went swimming one day,
   over the hill and far away.
   The mother duck said "Quack, quack, quack, quack",
   and only three little ducks came back.

3. Three little ducks went swimming one day,
   over the hill and far away.
   The mother duck said "Quack, quack, quack, quack",
   and only two little ducks came back.

4. Two little ducks went swimming one day,
   over the hill and far away.
   The mother duck said "Quack, quack, quack, quack",
   and only one little duck came back.

5. One little ducks went swimming one day,
   over the hill and far away.
   The mother duck said "Quack, quack, quack, quack",
   and all the five little ducks came back.

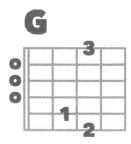

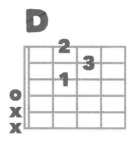

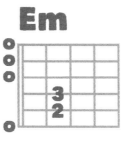

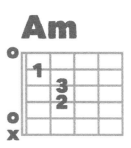

There was an old woman

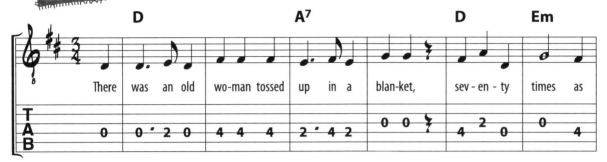

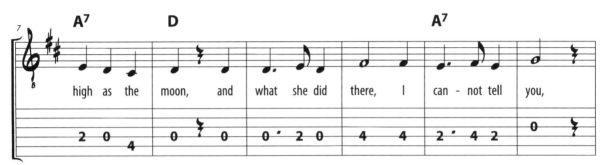

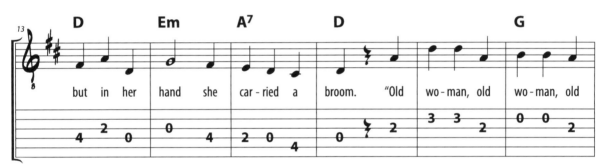

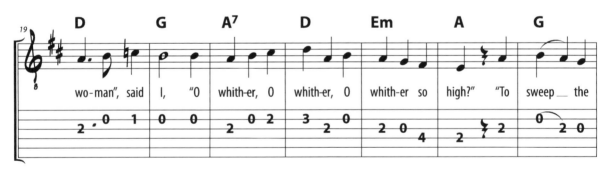

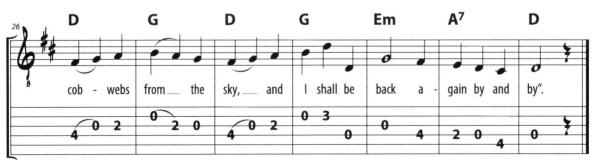

D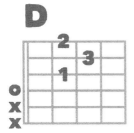

A⁷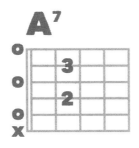

Em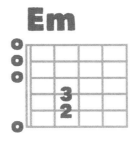

G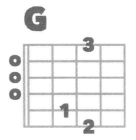

(How to read) Chord diagrams

Horizontal lines represent the strings of the guitar, vertical lines the frets.
The double line to the left of the diagram indicates the nut of your guitar.

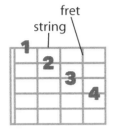

The fingers of the fretting hand are numbered 1-4:
1 = Index finger
2 = Middle finger
3 = Ringfinger
4 = Little finger (pinky)

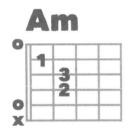

The chord symbol is given above the chord.

Open strings are indicated by an "0" to the left of the diagram, muted strings (strings that are not played or damped) by an "x".

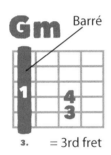

Fretboard positions are indicated below the chord.
If a chord is to be played as a so-called bar chord (i.e. fretting more than one string with the same finger) this is indicated by a black bar. The number inside the bar indicates the recommended fretting finger.

The Tablature

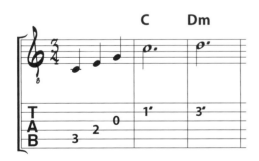

I've notated the songs' melodies in standard notation and tablature. If you can't read music, simply use the tablature. Here's how it's read: Horizontal lines represent the strings (with the 6th string at the bottom), while the numbers indicate the fret(s).
So the passage on the left reads: first play the A string, 3rd fret; followed by the D string, 2nd fret, followed by the G string played as an open string. For the next bar, play the B string, 2nd fret and for the third bar, play the B string, 3rd fret.

Tuning the guitar

The strings of the guitar are numbered 1-6 (starting with the one next to the floor).

1st string	=	e
2nd string	=	b
3rd string	=	G
4th string	=	D
5th string	=	A
6th string	=	E

- Tune the A string of your guitar using a reference pitch (piano, tuning fork or another already tuned guitar).
- Now play the E string (6th string) at the 5. fret, comparing its pitch to the open A string. Tune the E string until its pitch exactly matches that of the open A string.
- Play the A string at the 5. fret, comparing its pitch to the open D string. Change the open D strings' pitch until it exactly matches that of the A string played at the 5. fret.
- Play the D string at the 5. fret, comparing its pitch to the open G string. Change the open G strings' pitch until it exactly matches that of the D string played at the 5. fret.
- Play the G string at the (beware!) 4. fret, comparing its pitch to the open B string. Tune the B string until its pitch exactly matches that of the G string played at the 4. fret.
- Now play the B string at the 5. fret, comparing its pitch to the open E string. Change the open E strings' pitch until it exactly matches that of the B string played at the 5. fret.

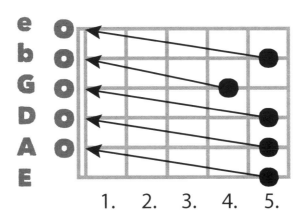

Of course, you can start tuning with any string you like. In the above example, I started with the A string because the note A is most often used as the reference pitch for tuning.

Learning to tune your guitar by ear can be frustrating because your hearing has to adapt to its new task, which will take some time. Buying an electronic tuner makes tuning accurate and hassle-free, but don't forget to tune your guitar by ear on a regular basis to learn this tuning method, too.

Strumming patterns

The following is a selection of basic strumming pattern which you can use for song accompaniment. These are just for starters - you'll soon use other, more elaborate pattern or invent your own. Feel free to use a pick or your finger(s) for strumming – basically whatever feels best.

Here's how they're read:

- The horizontal lines represent the strings of your guitar.
  Downstroke (strumming in the direction of the floor): arrow upward
  Upstroke: arrow downward.
- The length of the arrows indicates which strings to strum.
- Each of these pattern shows a whole measure.

For song accompaniment you can choose (and also combine) whatever pattern feels best to you, but keep in mind to match the pattern's time to the time of the song, e.g. for a song in 4/4 time only use strumming patterns in 4/4 time.
Songs in 2/2 time can be played using strumming patterns in 4/4 time.

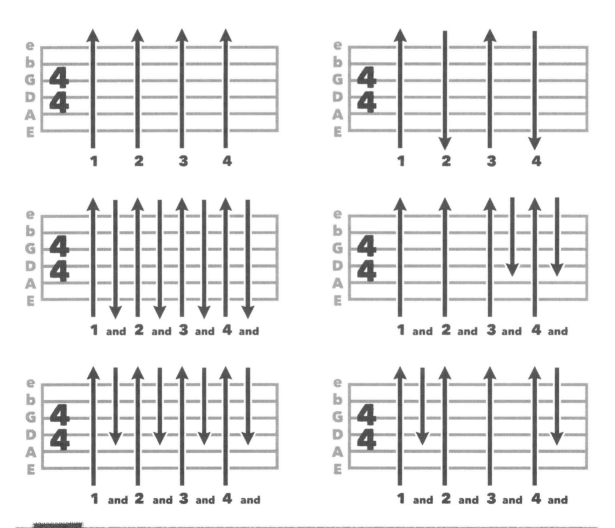

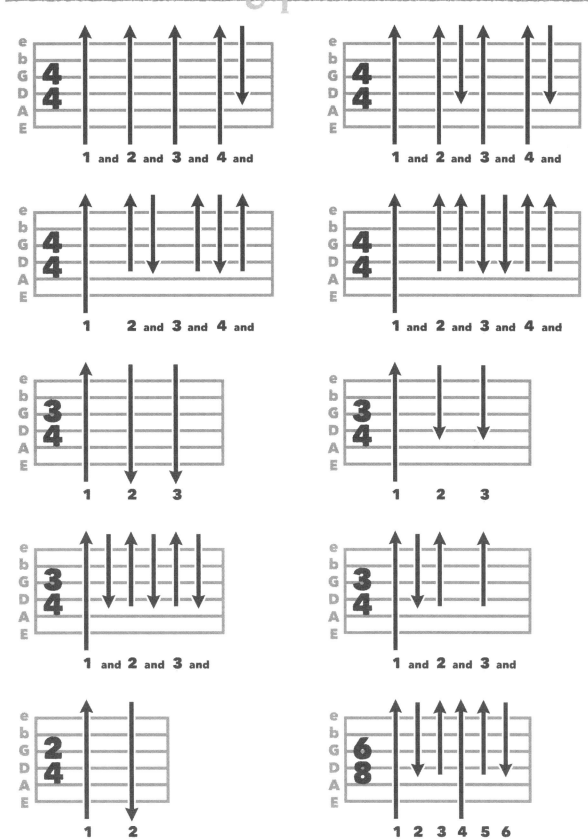

Picking patterns

A lot of songs sound particularly good when played using a picking pattern. Here's the basic idea: instead of picking all the notes of a chord simultaneously with you finger(s) or a pick, you play them successively, one after the other. Picking patterns are commonly used for longer musical sections (or even whole songs) and adapted to the chord changes if necessary. Here's an example, using the A minor chord:

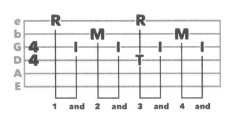

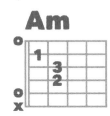

T = thumb
I = index finger
M = middle finger
R = ring finger

As in tablature, horizontal lines represent the strings of your guitar. The time signature is notated at the beginning of the pattern as a fraction (here: 4/4; this is a pattern for songs in 4/4 time). The letters T, I, M and R indicate the fingers of the picking hand. Below the pattern I've notated how to count it. Here's a step-by-step explanation of the above example:
- on the first beat ("1") the ring finger picks the e string.
- on the second half of the first beat ("1and") the index finger picks the G string.
- on the second beat ("2") the middle finger picks the b string.
- on the second half of the second beat ("2and") the index finger picks the G string once again.
- On the third beat, thumb and ring finger simultaneously pick the D and the e string.
and so on …

There are a few basic things to keep in mind when using picking patterns:
Obviously, the pattern's time signature has to match that of the song. In some cases, the pattern has to be adapted to a certain chord or a chord change, but most of the time you can use the following simple rule:
• pick the bass strings (6th, 5th and 4th) string with your thumb,
• pick the G (3rd) string with your index finger,
• the B (2nd) string with your middle finger and
• the e (1st) string with your ring finger.

One of the best ways to practise picking patterns is to play them on open strings until the movement of your fingers becomes second nature – practicing this way ensures you'll be able to concentrate on more important things when it's time to play the song.
When the picking pattern has been "automized" to a certain degree it's time to add chords and chord changes. Take your time because nothing sounds worse than a "stuttering" picking pattern interfering with a smooth chord change.
On the following pages you'll find some basic picking patterns to choose from. Of course, this is just a small selection from the multitude of possible patterns, meant to whet your appetite – you'll soon find varying patterns and inventing new ones of your own can be lots of fun!

For a start, you may want to try:
• Combining different picking patterns
  (e. g. one for the verse and one for the chorus).
• Combining picking patterns with strumming patterns.
• Mixing picking patterns with melody lines and damping techniques.
• Playing some of your favorites "backwards".

Sometimes you'll encounter indications in Spanish:
P (pulgar) = thumb
I (indice) = index finger
M (medio) = middle finger
A (anular) = ring finger

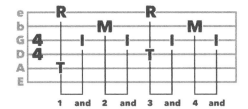

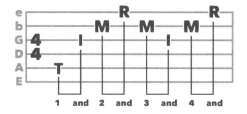

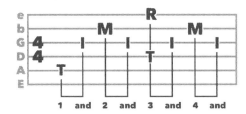

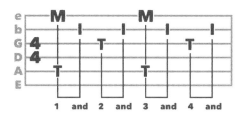

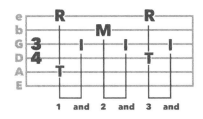

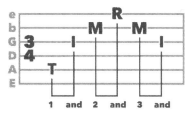

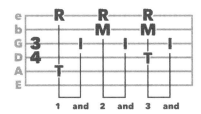

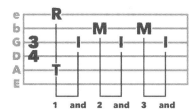

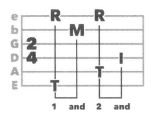

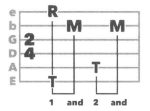

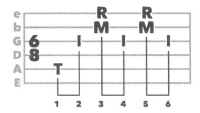

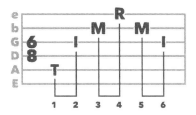

Basic chords

On the following pages I've compiled the chords used in this book. Naturally, this chord collection is far from complete – there are literally thousands of guitar chords (some common, some pretty obscure). If you want to expand your chord repertoire (or simply look up a chord you don't know), a chord chart is always a wise investment, and of course you can find almost any guitar chord on the internet.

Depending on the musical context, some chords may have more than one name:

$$C\sharp = D\flat, \quad D\sharp = E\flat, \quad F\sharp = G\flat, \quad G\sharp = A\flat \quad \text{und} \quad A\sharp = B\flat$$

For guitar players this simply means: C$\sharp$ and D$\flat$ are played the same and they sound the same. If, for example, you happen to stumble upon a G$\sharp$m (G sharp minor) chord, don't worry: just play A$\flat$m.

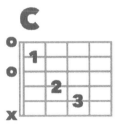
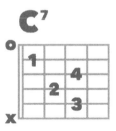
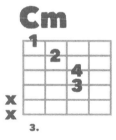
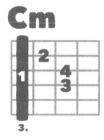

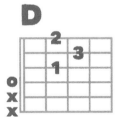
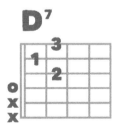
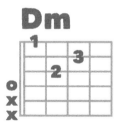
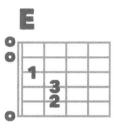

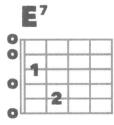
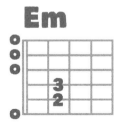
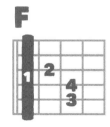
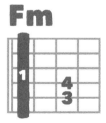

F♯m

G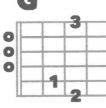

G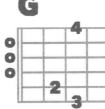

G⁷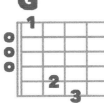

Gm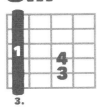

A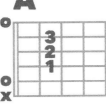

A⁷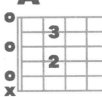

Am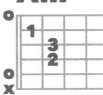

B♭

B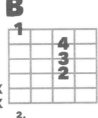

B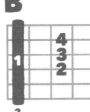

B⁷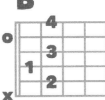

Bm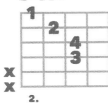

Bm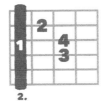

Made in the USA
Monee, IL
16 October 2021